THE AUTISM SPECTRUM AND
DEPRESSION

by the same author

Asperger Syndrome and Anxiety
A Guide to Successful Stress Management
Foreword by Valerie Gaus
ISBN 978 1 84310 895 5
eISBN 978 1 84642 922 4

Asperger Syndrome and Bullying
Strategies and Solutions
Foreword by Michael John Carley
ISBN 978 1 84310 846 7
eISBN 978 1 84642 635 3

Asperger Syndrome and Employment
A Personal Guide to Succeeding at Work (DVD)
With Gail Hawkins
ISBN 978 1 84310 849 8

Being Bullied
Strategies and Solutions for People with Asperger's Syndrome (DVD)
ISBN 978 1 84310 843 6

The Autism Spectrum, Sexuality and the Law
Tony Attwood, Isabelle Henault and Nick Dubin
ISBN 978 1 84905 919 0
eISBN 978 0 85700 679 0

THE AUTISM SPECTRUM AND
DEPRESSION

N I C K   D U B I N

Jessica Kingsley *Publishers*
London and Philadelphia

First published in 2014
by Jessica Kingsley Publishers
73 Collier Street
London N1 9BE, UK
and
400 Market Street, Suite 400
Philadelphia, PA 19106, USA

www.jkp.com

Copyright © Nick Dubin 2014
Foreword copyright © Tony Attwood 2014

Library of Congress Cataloging in Publication Data
A CIP catalog record for this book is available from the Library of Congress

British Library Cataloguing in Publication Data
A CIP catalogue record for this book is available from the British Library

ISBN 978 1 84905 814 8
eISBN 978 0 85700 242 6

Printed and bound in Great Britain

To Dr. S and Julia

Contents

Foreword by Tony Attwood   11

ACKNOWLEDGMENTS   13

Introduction   15

1   The Relationship between the Autism Spectrum and
    Depression   25

2   Defining Depression   49

3   Cognitive–Behavioral Therapy   81

4   The Dark Night of the Soul   113

5   Suicide is the Forever Decision   133

6   Perfectionism and Depression   139

7   Anger and Depression   147

8   Managing Depression   155

9   Interview with My Parents   187

    AFTERWORD   203

    APPENDIX I: A LIST OF RECOMMENDED BOOKS   205

    APPENDIX II: ASPIE SELF-CHECK LIST   207

    REFERENCES   215

    INDEX   219

Foreword

Almost 75 percent of adults who have Asperger syndrome[1] are vulnerable to feeling sad, but about a third of children and adults with Asperger syndrome have the clear signs of a clinical depression. While psychologists, parents, and people with Asperger syndrome have long recognized the propensity for brief episodes of intense sadness and prolonged feelings of depression, there has been a conspicuous lack of literature on the reasons why, or practical suggestions regarding what can be done to alleviate this depression. At last we have Nick Dubin's book, which is the seminal publication on depression and Asperger syndrome. As a clinician, I was impressed with his understanding and explanation of the theoretical models of depression and how the models apply to the life experiences of someone with Asperger syndrome.

The reasons why a person who has Asperger syndrome can feel depressed include low self-esteem due to being ridiculed, bullied, and rejected by peers, the mental exhaustion from trying to succeed socially, feeling desperately lonely, chronic and prolonged anxiety, believing and internalizing criticism from family members and

---

1   A separate diagnostic category of Asperger syndrome is not included in the clinician's diagnostic manual, DSM-5, which was published in 2013. The term Asperger syndrome is replaced with the new diagnostic term, Autism Spectrum Disorder Level 1. However, the term Asperger syndrome, which has been in general usage for over two decades, will still be used legitimately by clinicians, parents, teachers, therapists, and those with an ASD Level 1. The general public will also continue to use the term in conversations, as will the media. For consistency and simplicity, the term Asperger syndrome is used throughout this book.

peers, and empathic sensitivity to the suffering of others. Nick Dubin describes strategies to increase optimism, improve self-esteem, constructively express negative emotions, and engage in positive social experiences.

The book is eminently readable with an engaging style, and includes examples from the author's personal experiences. The text provides insight into the causes and treatment of depression, but also provides an opportunity for the reader to contemplate how the new knowledge can be applied in his or her own life. Some of the author's comments are so perceptive: for example, "I have never met anyone with Asperger's who was depressed when he was involved with a special interest."

The Autism Spectrum and Depression will be my primary reference book for explanations and ideas to alleviate depression for clients in my clinical practice. I also suggest that it should be recommended reading for someone who has Asperger syndrome, and also for families and fellow clinicians. If you are feeling depressed because you have Asperger syndrome, or know someone with Asperger syndrome who seems depressed, please buy and read this book.

Tony Attwood, Ph.D.
Clinical Psychologist, Minds & Hearts Clinic, Australia

Acknowledgments

Special thanks to Katie Kramer for her deep and abiding friendship, and to my parents for their never-ending love and support.

Introduction

Depression has been around since the dawn of mankind, yet over the past 50 years there has been an epidemic rise in this condition as well as an explosion of treatments and approaches to try to cope with it. Medication, psychotherapy, muscle relaxation techniques, meditation, biofeedback, and hypnosis are a just a few of the options that attempt to alleviate or cure the symptoms of depression. Despite the availability of all these treatments, many people are still profoundly depressed.

Unfortunately, depression is still a taboo subject. Although the media and society have focused a lot of attention on it, family members and friends of those who are depressed often have trouble discussing this issue. Those closest to someone who is depressed will often ignore the problem, hoping it will just go away. This demonstrable lack of interest only furthers the self-loathing a depressed person feels. In essence, the message being sent is: feeling depressed is your fault, and if you would only pick yourself up by your bootstraps, you would get better. The depressed person internalizes this message. Friends and family are often unintentionally insensitive, saying things like, "Are you still down? It's been a month already," indicating that the person should be over it by now.

Because depressed people generally blame themselves for their condition, they are embarrassed and reluctant to ask for help. Despite all the famous people who have publicly acknowledged that they have suffered with depression, there is still a certain stigma associated with mental illness, particularly depression. People still believe that being strong is the ability to deal with problems on your own, when the truth is that strong people ask for help when they need it.

What does the subject of depression have to do with Asperger syndrome (AS)? As someone who has been depressed at certain times in my life, I became interested in this subject long before I was diagnosed Asperger's. My interest was beyond academic. I wondered about my mental condition and why I was so unhappy so much of the time. I asked myself questions such as, "Why am I so depressed? What could be causing these dark moods? Why do other people appear to be happy and enjoying life? Why am I different?" I hoped that in time introspection and my academic studies in psychology would answer these questions.

Ten years ago, when I was diagnosed with Asperger syndrome at the age of 27, I began to question whether there was a connection between Asperger's and depression. Since that time, I have come to some important conclusions through research, cognitive–behavioral therapy, my own life experience, as well as meeting hundreds of people on the autism spectrum. Most important, I have learned that depression is not only connected to one's psychological status, but it can also be a by-product of neurological differences.

In my last book, *Asperger Syndrome and Anxiety* (2009), I explored the relationship between those two conditions and offered strategies to cope successfully with the stress that can result from them. It was the first book of its kind. Because it received such a positive response from both critics and readers, Jessica Kingsley Publishers asked that my next book investigate the connection between Asperger syndrome and depression. Understanding the correlation between Asperger's and anxiety makes it easier to manage stress. Similarly, recognizing the link between Asperger's and depression aims to achieve a parallel goal.

What if a person with diabetes, in the hopes of getting advice about healthy eating, bought a book on nutrition that was written for the general public? The advice and suggestions in that book could be misguiding or perhaps even harmful to someone with diabetes. In the same respect, someone with Asperger's who is hoping to benefit from a book on depression that does not take Asperger's into account might not receive the appropriate guidance. Having Asperger syndrome causes a person to view the world from different sensory, emotional, and cultural viewpoints. If these viewpoints are not taken into consideration, it would be like the person with diabetes going on a high-carbohydrate diet following the advice read in a general book on nutrition.

It is important to understand why depression and Asperger's are so deeply intertwined. First, the world of Asperger's can be quite complex, confusing, and emotionally exhausting for the individual with this neurological condition. But neurological wiring isn't always the direct cause of depression. The real cause can often be how others respond to these neurological differences. Consider this: if having Asperger syndrome were the norm, the chances are that fewer people with this neurological difference would be depressed. A major source of negative energy for those with Asperger's (also referred to as Aspies) is the constant pressure to try to fit in with the general public and the continual failure to do so. Although many people can identify with the issue of not fitting in, those with Asperger's suffer much more intensely because of their differences. The need to act as neurotypically as possible in order to appear normal is a pervasive struggle for people with Asperger's. Situations in which they constantly have to be on guard are present in all aspects of their lives, from personal relationships to employment, to the seemingly mundane aspects of daily interactions. The problem with trying to act like a neurotypical person is that it can be mentally and physically exhausting to keep up the act since it doesn't come naturally.

There are many reasons why people with Asperger's can experience depression. Even though they share a common diagnosis, they are still unique individuals who cannot be pigeonholed into any one set of behaviors. One of the maxims of the neurodiversity movement, which believes neurological differences should be respected not judged, is "If you've met one person on the autism spectrum, you've met one person on the autism spectrum." This statement encapsulates the belief that no two people with Asperger's are alike. I have been disheartened by the general literature on depression because most of it does not include the specific issues of those with Asperger's and usually emphasizes only one the following modalities and treatments:

- biological or physiological causes with nutritional and medication treatments

- psychological causes with cognitive–behavioral therapy

- environmental causes with appropriate remedies

- psychodynamic causes with a clinical approach to one's personality development.

Rather than focus exclusively on any one of these components, I will utilize a "bio-psychosocial" approach in this book—an integrative examination into depression and Asperger's incorporating these key modalities.

People with Asperger's often feel alone, alienated, and depressed. My goal in writing this book is to give hope, to provide knowledge, and to offer ways to cope with depression. I strongly believe that depression can provide fertile soil for personal growth. Like any other challenge in life, depression can present an opportunity for self-understanding and new awareness.

Although I probably started having symptoms of depression as early as elementary school, I didn't actually recognize them as such until much later. One episode of depression that stands out took place when I was in high school. I had been asked to work as a tennis instructor at a country club one summer in a wealthy Detroit suburb. I was ecstatic. This seemed like the perfect job for me. I had been playing tennis ever since I was eight years old, and it was the only activity in my life at which I excelled. I was not doing particularly well in school, I didn't have many friends, and tennis was my primary source of self-esteem. I lived, ate, and breathed tennis. When I wasn't actually playing the game, I was watching reruns of old matches on television or reading books about the sport.

I knew every fact there was to know about the history of tennis. I could tell you which players were in every Grand Slam tournament going back 20 years, and I knew the exact scores of each match. In short, tennis was my life.

Even though I was a skilled player, I knew I could never play professionally because of my height. I was—and still am—five foot six. My plan was to make a career of teaching tennis, and this country club job would be a great start toward that career. One of the prerequisites of becoming a tennis professional is earning United States Professional Tennis Association (USPTA) certification. Even though the country club job did not require it, I decided to get this certification because I knew I would need it someday. I studied hard over the next several months and was thrilled when I passed the written exam and the practical skills test, thereby earning my USPTA certificate. I was on my way!

I remember feeling great the first day on the job. The sky was a bright blue and the sun was shining. I arrived at the club and took in the whole view: the gorgeous landscaping, the well-dressed members, and the beautifully maintained tennis courts. I felt like I really belonged here. But despite this wonderful feeling, it wasn't that long before things started to go wrong.

First, there were the social aspects of the job. All the other pros joked around with one another and had an easy camaraderie. Somehow, I felt apart from these other employees. They enjoyed getting together after work and going to bars to relax and have a beer, but I had no interest in doing that. Of course, I didn't understand the reasons for my social unease, this being about ten years prior to receiving my Asperger's diagnosis. Then there were the club members themselves. The other pros seemed to know instinctively what to say to them and how to persuade them to take lessons. Again, I felt like the odd man out, as I usually got tongue-tied whenever I tried socializing with the members. There was no way I was going to try to convince any of them to take a lesson from me. That was *way* out of my comfort zone.

My weak fine motor skills presented another difficulty. I struggled with tasks like stringing racquets, setting up the nets, and drawing the lines on the court. I also had trouble with multitasking, like when my boss would give me a number of chores to do at the same time.

But the biggest problem I had at that job was my immediate superior, an arrogant man whom I will call Bill. He immediately sensed my vulnerability and played it like a Stradivarius violin. He made fun of me in front of the children I was teaching and referred to me as "The Waddler" because of the way I tended to walk with my feet pointing outward. One day Bill gathered some of the kids I was teaching and as a "joke" locked me in the men's bathroom. I was mortified. I kept pounding on the door asking for help, and I could hear all of them laughing at me right outside the door. I will never forget that day. I had been bullied at school, but I certainly didn't expect to be bullied at work. I couldn't believe Bill had done this to me, and yet it never even occurred to me to report his inappropriate behavior to *his* superior.

What began as my dream job quickly turned into a living nightmare. I didn't hit it off with the other pros, had trouble socializing with the club members, felt Bill had taken away any respect my students might have had for me, and made me look foolish in their eyes. But there was no way out. Every day I came home from the club feeling more and more depressed. Not only was I unsuccessful at what I thought was going to be a great summer job, but it also started to dawn on me that becoming a tennis pro was not a viable career path. That realization was devastating and triggered a depression that lasted throughout the summer. Unfortunately, it would not be my last bout of depression.

The world is fraught with injustices, both real and imagined. Our lives can make us feel that we are in a continuous uphill struggle with no relief in sight. For some, the deck is stacked against us from birth. The causes for our suffering can be numerous: economic conditions, physical or mental disabilities, discrimination, a dysfunctional family life, disease, abuse, and so on. Any of these circumstances can create an ongoing feeling of despair. Even if we don't have specific hardships, the precarious state of the world is always there as a potential source of unhappiness.

If anyone looks hard enough, he or she can find reasons for being depressed. Certainly those on the autism spectrum would have no problem justifying their depression. But if earth is a boot camp, I believe those with Asperger's are all warriors in training. Having depression *and* Asperger's are definitely two major obstacles in life. However, the great Helen Keller once said that the soul comes to grow through trial and suffering. That is a profound statement for someone who had such severe disabilities. She lived in a world of silence and darkness but was still able to become one of the most respected individuals of the twentieth century. What if Helen Keller had given up when her teacher Annie Sullivan persisted in trying to connect the word "water" with the tapping on Helen's hand? She would have likely lived a depressed life in utter darkness. But Helen Keller's determination and grit not only made her one of the most respected persons who ever lived, but also permitted her to live an extremely rich and meaningful life. It is precisely because she could not see or hear that she was able to teach the rest of humanity to open its eyes and ears. Her path in life was obviously far more difficult than most, but one could justifiably argue that her lifetime of psychological and spiritual growth was just as remarkable as her cognitive development.

Viktor Frankl, the famous Holocaust survivor, is another example of someone who faced great hardships and yet was able to live a purposeful life. In his brilliant book *Man's Search for Meaning* (1959), he described how he was able to survive the physical and mental torture of years in a Nazi death camp. He explained how he experienced meaning in his life under the worst possible circumstances. He went on to write several international best sellers and became one of the most prominent existential philosophers of the last century. Clearly, the incredible obstacles that he and Helen Keller were forced to confront helped them achieve their greatness rather than their destruction.

The tougher the circumstances one has to overcome, the greater the potential rewards. Under the right conditions and with the appropriate support, anyone can strive to emulate people like Viktor Frankl and Helen Keller and become the unsung heroes of their own lives. Everyone has the potential to change from a helpless victim into a resilient warrior. This book will encourage readers not to let depression diminish their enthusiasm for life, but instead to make use of their Asperger's or autistic traits in order to live the best and most meaningful life possible.

Life is about risk and reward. The stock market is a perfect example of this principle. The more one invests, the greater the potential for financial reward, and yes, the more an investor stands to lose. Paradoxically speaking, I would contend there is a greater risk in *not* trying to manage one's depression than in simply being a malcontent. What I am advocating is for people to embrace a certain amount of risk. Stepping outside of one's comfort zone is necessary in order to cope with depression. Although this strategy may create a higher risk of failure, the rewards are definitely worth it.

Contrary to what some believe, depression is not the natural way for those with Asperger's to live. Aspies are generally energetic people who take pride in their achievements. They become passionately invested in life when they pursue their interests and exercise their intellect. They tend to thrive when they feel they can contribute to society, be useful, and live life on their own terms. I have never met anyone with Asperger's who was depressed when he was involved with a special interest. Aspies tend to hyperfocus on certain subjects from which they derive great satisfaction (but which may not interest others). However, when they get depressed they lose the incentive to seek appropriate stimulation from activities that bring them joy. When depression strikes, they become lethargic and lose their zest for life.

Usually when I feel depressed, I can temporarily lift myself out of it by engaging in one of my special interests, such as watching or playing tennis or listening to jazz or classical music. When I was working at the country club, however, my depression was so severe, I was unable to access the pleasure those activities normally provided.

There are two caveats to keep in mind when reading this book. First, any advice or suggestions I offer are not intended to replace the professional treatment and care a therapist, psychiatrist, or any other mental health professional may provide. Second, this book is not a primer on Asperger's. I am making the assumption that most readers have a basic knowledge of the subject. If the reader needs any additional information, I would recommend Tony Attwood's *The Complete Guide to Asperger Syndrome* (2008).

Now that I've taken care of the preliminaries, let the journey begin.

Chapter 1

The Relationship between the Autism Spectrum and Depression

Many of you may be familiar with the inspiring story of Siddhartha, a spiritual teacher from ancient India who founded Buddhism. In this classic tale, a baby boy was born in the foothills of the Himalayas, several hundred years before the birth of Christ. This was not any ordinary infant. He was a prince of the kingdom called Shakya, in what is today southern Nepal. The king and queen of Shakya had been trying to conceive a child in order to have an heir. With the birth of their son, they succeeded. They decided to name their baby Siddhartha, which translates to "every wish fulfilled." Since they achieved their wish to become parents, the king decided to make sure his son's every wish would also be fulfilled.

As Siddhartha grew up he was sheltered and protected due to his father's efforts. He was essentially a captive within his own palace. Guards were stationed all around the palace to prevent him from leaving the premises. As a consolation for his lack of freedom, young Siddhartha was treated to the finest things in life. He had the best teachers, the most wonderful food, and many loyal friends. It's hard to imagine anyone in contemporary society being as sheltered from the real world as young Siddhartha was.

Siddhartha eventually paid a price for his long-held captivity. He yearned to experience life beyond the palace gates and was bored with his perfect life. Much of his restlessness was understandable, for deep down he sensed that there was more to the world and more to life than what appeared within his utopian existence.

One day Siddhartha was sitting under an apple tree and saw fields being plowed to make way for next year's crops. In the process, he noticed that several insects in the field had died. This was his first realization of death and the notion of possible suffering. The whole concept puzzled him. He had never been exposed to anything negative in his young life, so to see these insects lying lifeless on the ground actually infused him with a sense of empathy and compassion toward these creatures. These were feelings he had never experienced before. This episode foreshadowed how he would feel when he left the palace for the first time as a young adult.

He was in his late 20s when he first left the palace. It was his persistent pleading that finally convinced his father to let him see the outside world. In wanting his son to be happy and observing his son's frustration over being confined, the king gave in to young Siddhartha's wishes. The prince was in for quite a shock on his first venture outside of the palace gates. For when he left the palace grounds, he came upon a very old man. Seeing someone this old was also a new experience for him. He was naively unaware that people grow old, lose their faculties, and often endure suffering as they age. This new awareness deeply troubled the prince. He now understood that growing older would eventually happen to him. How could he possibly enjoy his life knowing that someday he might have to endure this kind of suffering?

After having more experiences in the world, the prince came to realize that real life wasn't as perfect as it seemed to be in the palace. This realization brought Siddhartha into a deep, dark depression. His palace, which was supposed to be an ideal environment for him, was now an agonizingly disturbing place. How could he possibly enjoy everything around him when there was so much suffering going on in the outside world? As a consequence of this depression, Siddhartha did the only thing that made sense to him. He decided *he* had to experience some suffering too. Not just half-heartedly, but to an extreme. He chose to become an ascetic. By renouncing all his worldly desires and possessions, he believed that he could attain enlightenment. He starved himself, went without proper clothes or shelter, and slept on uncomfortable surfaces. Ultimately, Siddhartha learned that none of this suffering brought him the enlightenment he was seeking. So what did the prince decide to do? He meditated under the famous Bodhi tree and awakened to become the enlightened Buddha.

The first time I read this story of the young prince who was transformed into an enlightened being, I identified intensely with him, not just on a personal level, but also as someone with Asperger's. The part I identified with the most was Siddhartha's first childlike realization that the world involves suffering, both natural and manmade. Like Siddhartha, I felt overprotected when I was growing up. Even though I had not yet been diagnosed with Asperger's, my parents recognized certain traits in me like naivete, gullibility, and difficulty socializing, which are typical in Asperger's children. Because of these qualities, they tried to protect me as much as possible. As I grew up and began to experience more of the world, like Siddhartha, I became increasingly attuned to suffering and injustice. It seemed to me that rather than fighting injustice, most people were more concerned with accumulating material possessions and chose to ignore the social ills that were all around them.

While people with Asperger's are not perceived to be empathetic, I strongly believe that they are very sensitive to the suffering of others. They are unquestionably concerned with issues of social justice on a grand scale. I have met many people with Asperger's and almost every one of them is deeply affected by unfairness and injustice.

The Lure of Depressive Realism

I used to be a committed pessimist, insisting that the world was a terribly cruel and absurd (to borrow from existentialist Albert Camus) place to live. That view reinforced the alienation I felt toward my surroundings. Philosophers refer to this view as depressive realism. Dr. Peter Kramer (2005) suggests that this perspective, taken to the extreme, can be self-defeating but also very alluring. For some, seeing the world as a terrible place can provide a hidden benefit. The more alienated people feel from their surroundings, the more pride they can take in their unique view of the world. In other words, depressive realism can almost become a source of joy because an individual can feel superior for observing life's absurdities that others fail to see. In this way, depression and cynicism can have an enticing quality. For example, if I know that I'm living in a corrupt world but no one else can understand it to the degree that I do, it must mean I possess great wisdom. This "wisdom" performs two functions: it supports the value of being depressed, and it helps to counteract feelings of low self-esteem. Depressive realism can make people feel superior if it allows them to perceive others as inferior for not seeing what is obviously true. Lord Byron described pessimism as a "fearful gift" and "the telescope of truth" (Cohen 1995). Leo Tolstoy compared depressive realism to being sober after awakening from a drunken state. He claimed that once sober, the senses are no longer dulled from alcohol and that life returns to being a cruel, absurd joke. In essence, these two writers are saying the same thing: the primary benefit of depressive realism is that it helps to keep us on guard against the painful realities of life. But is that benefit real or illusory?

People who constantly reflect on the misery of the human condition but avoid experience in the real world tend to be tortured souls (Cohen 1995). Seeing only the suffering of humanity is what drove the Buddha into his initial state of depression.

The energies of pessimism are fueled by guardedness and an abundance of caution. This attitude is what keeps people from pursuing their dreams and interests. In a pessimistic state, one expects bad things to happen simply because they have happened so many times in the past, whether these bad things are of a personal nature or on a global scale. On a personal level, I know a woman who has decided not to travel anywhere because she once went on a trip to Jamaica on which the airline lost her luggage and there was a major tropical storm the week she was there. When people ask her why she never travels she says, "Why leave home? It's just asking for trouble."

On a more global scale, the energies of pessimism were on display during the 2008 presidential election in the United States. There was quite a debate around the issue of relations with Iran. Barack Obama believed that there should be an effort to try to communicate with that nation, while other candidates took a different and perhaps more cynical viewpoint, insisting that there should be no effort to communicate because Iran could never be trusted.

Empathetic Attunement

One theory as to why people with Asperger's are hyper-attuned to suffering and social inequities is because they are a minority population. As a general rule, minorities tend to experience more difficulty and stress in their lives. For example, African-Americans have to cope with people often judging them on the color of their skin rather than for who they really are. Similarly, those with Asperger's can also be perceived in a one dimensional way as being weird or different rather than as multi-facted individuals.

I know a man who is African-American and has Asperger's. He has told me on numerous occasions that being a double minority has made him highly sensitive to the pain and misfortune of others. In addition to the overt discrimination he has faced as a black man, he has also had to navigate through life as an Aspie in an often impatient, intolerant, and conforming world. Being a double minority not only makes him a perennial outsider, but also provides him with personal insight and experience into the pain inflicted by his fellow man. One might assume that having these two strikes against him would be enough to crush his spirit. On the contrary, instead of making him a pessimist, it has made him more compassionate. He has used his empathic energy constructively and effectively to start a nonprofit organization specifically aimed at reducing the financial costs incurred by individuals with autism and their families. His hyper-attunement to suffering does not lead to pessimism or being a victim. Rather, he leads an active life of compassion.

The notion of Aspies being hypersensitive to the mistreatment and misfortune of others goes against conventional theory that they lack the capacity to be empathetic. In fact, Aspies are extremely empathetic people who often have a hard time outwardly demonstrating that feeling. Different people express the same emotion in different ways. For instance, I always knew my grandfather loved me, but he had difficulty showing that love either in words or in physical actions. He was uncomfortable saying "I love you," and didn't hug me very often, but I could feel his love. He just didn't know how to show affection as other grandparents might. The same can be true with people who have Asperger's. They feel the feelings but don't always know how to show them.

Like the African-American man with Asperger's, I am a member of several minority groups. I have Asperger's, I'm Jewish and I'm gay. While I was growing up, other kids bullied or made fun of me because of all these differences. They made fun of my clumsiness, the way I sometimes talked like a "little professor," and the way I paced around the room to keep my energy in check. Also, I was one of only two Jewish children in my grade in elementary school. On several occasions, my classmates made anti-Semitic remarks to me. But the most painful kind of bullying I experienced was in middle school where I was mercilessly teased as a result of what others perceived to be my sexual orientation. This is a common experience for adolescents with Asperger's who are often seen as gay, whether they are or not, due to their lack of social experience. At the time I was very confused about my sexuality and the bullying only intensified that confusion. Being a minority in these different ways has given me a broad insight into the life of the outsider and has taught me some important life lessons. I've experienced firsthand how unfairly people can treat others who are different or a minority and the pain of discrimination.

Personal and Positional Identifications

Social psychologists recognize that over-identification with others can fall into two categories: the personal and the positional (Van Zomeren and Lodewijkx 2009). Personal identification occurs when one identifies with another person's struggles. Positional identification refers to identifying with a whole group of people that one does not know personally, but who have been treated unjustly. As I mentioned, I am Jewish. The Jewish people are a strong and unified group, in part because of their history of persecution. An example of a positional identification would be if every time I heard of a Jewish person being discriminated against, I might become fearful that this could also happen to me. Similarly, learning that someone with AS has been wronged in some way could trigger the same type of reaction. Members of minorities or groups that are mistreated have to guard against their compassion morphing into an all-consuming fear about how these injustices could someday happen to them.

If I feel empathy toward my friend because she studied hard for her final exam but ended up failing it, that would be an example of personal identification. My empathy does not extend beyond my friend to a categorical imperative such as "No one should ever fail a final exam." However, if I see a homeless man pushing a shopping cart with his belongings in it, and feel sad that he doesn't have a place to live, my empathy may extend beyond that person. My categorical position could be "No one should ever be homeless."

Researchers have found that positional identifications were the strongest when it was more difficult to blame the victims for their suffering (Lerner 1980). In the case of my friend who failed her exam, it could easily be assumed that if she had tried a different method of study or prepared harder, she might have had a better chance of passing the exam. Most people would think that there is nothing inherently wrong with a professor failing a student on an exam, because the student has to take responsibility for learning the material. However, the homeless man would present a different analysis. A compassionate person might reasonably believe that there is no reason why *any* human being should be homeless—that no amount of laziness, ineptitude, or societal circumstances should ever justify anyone having to live on the streets. That would be an example of positional identification-based empathy. It is fair to say the issues with which we most empathize are those with which we personally identify.

Positional identifications can be quite strong within minority populations. Group identities coalesce when those with similar or identical struggles feel the need to unite for a common cause. "We the people," "We shall overcome," and "Workers of the World, Unite!" are slogans that reflect this type of group solidarity. Positional identifications within the Asperger's community have been solidified and strengthened with the advent of the Internet, the favorite means of communication for Aspies. Today, this population has evolved into a strong group identity.

The iconography of the Asperger's landscape has shifted dramatically in the past two decades. Twenty years ago an adult with Asperger's would likely have been misdiagnosed because the AS diagnosis did not exist at that time. Like many others who grew up without a correct diagnosis, I was misdiagnosed with attention deficit disorder (ADD) and certain learning disabilities. In 1994, with the diagnosis of Asperger syndrome firmly established in the *Diagnostic and Statistical Manual of Mental Disorders* (*DSM-IV*), people with this condition finally came to know themselves and began to make their stories public in the form of first-person accounts, books, on the Internet, and through social meetings. This development did wonders for the ability to build empathetic bridges among Aspies who had similar struggles. This process of greater communication also helped to create several Aspie-run Internet sites and a number of self-advocacy autism organizations around the world. These positional identifications had the effect of making people with Asperger's no longer feel alone in the world. For the first time in their lives, this existential feeling of isolation was seemingly eliminated overnight.

Suddenly, the perennial outsiders were transformed into important insiders. I believe this collective discovery has been one of the most effective remedies for depression for the entire Asperger's community.

There is one downside to this solidarity. Many with AS have so strongly identified with the overarching struggles of this group that they have neglected their own individual interests and needs. I have a colleague and friend who wrote her doctoral dissertation on the special interests of those with Asperger's. She interviewed 12 people regarding their special interests and, more often than not, the interviewees used the pronoun "we" rather than "I" when referring to themselves. In essence, some of these Aspies had become so subsumed within the collective identity that the line had blurred between their individual and group identities. Jerry Newport, one of the first people with Asperger's to make his story public, wisely stated, "Life is not a label." This is an excellent reminder not to sacrifice individuality to a group identity.

Another danger of becoming subsumed within a collective through positional identification is that it can lead to taking on the fears and frustrations of others. I have met many individuals with Asperger's who are employed but who feel guilty that many other Aspies are not. While this may be a compassionate response, it can undermine the self-esteem that comes from one's own achievements. It's something like survivor's guilt. How can I be happy when members of my group are still suffering?

To paraphrase the self-development author and speaker Wayne Dyer, no amount of feeling bad for others will actually benefit them unless you take direct action to help them. Similarly, no amount of feeling bad for others will help *you* feel any better. This doesn't mean you should be selfish or insensitive to the inequities of others, but allowing a positional identification to depress you is counterproductive and even self-destructive.

Altrusim

Another reason why people with Asperger's are especially sensitive to the suffering of others is their belief that they can change the world. Some might call this grandiosity. Although changing the world might be unrealistic, it seems to be an extreme response to injustice based on a life experience of continual alienation and mistreatment. The Asperger's Association of New England website (2013) states, "For unknown reasons, it is particularly common for people with Asperger's to feel a deep concern for human welfare, animal rights, environmental protection, and other global and humanitarian causes."

Remember, the Buddha's initial depression was triggered by the discovery of the world's imperfections and how he would inevitably suffer from those negative consequences if he lived long enough. At first, the Buddha tried to ward off his depression by denying himself any of the world's pleasures, and this cemented his decision to become an ascetic. However, he quickly discovered that this path did not bring him the enlightenment he was seeking. Asceticism did not provide the refuge from the world's suffering he thought it would. He ultimately discovered that despite his great concern for the injustice of others, no amount of personal pain could alleviate human suffering. So after meditating under the Bodhi tree, the Buddha eventually acquired the wisdom that he would derive the greatest happiness when being of service to others. Along with other great teachers and prophets, the Buddha shares this recipe for happiness with the world.

Research has convincingly demonstrated that altruism can be a powerful force in combating depression. The data shows that if a person's attention is significantly focused on helping others, his or her level of healthy altruism will lead to greater personal satisfaction (Morris and Kanfer 1983). Conversely, a person who is depressed will most likely have an unhealthy level of altruism. It is interesting to note that depressives usually have higher aspirations for wanting to be altruistic but are hindered by immobility caused by their depression (Morris and Kanfer 1983). This failure to act on their altruistic impulses produces a deep sense of guilt. Depression not only blocks altruistic actions, it also creates passivity and helplessness. A vicious cycle comes into play causing more feelings of worthlessness and shame, which reinforce feelings of depression.

It is hard to muster the strength to get out of bed, let alone be altruistic, when one is depressed. Taking a shower or even brushing one's teeth in the morning becomes a chore. Those who are depressed frequently stay home from work, thus losing personal income as well as costing the economy millions of dollars each year. Depression is debilitating and draining and makes it difficult, if not impossible, to reach out to others.

It is important for people with Asperger's to be aware of their need to help others and how depression can frustrate meeting that need. One way to become more altruistic is to identify an activity that would benefit other people. For example, if you are concerned with senior citizens who may be lonely and not adequately cared for (perhaps because you worry that you won't be properly cared for at that age), then visit a senior residence center and ask if there is any volunteer work you can perform. In acting on your desire to improve the lives of senior citizens, you will not only be actualizing your concern for others, but you will also feel better about yourself.

Perhaps you are concerned about abandoned dogs or cats not getting the love they deserve or even being euthanized if a home is not found for them. Consider volunteering at a local animal shelter or adopting a dog or cat. There are many known psychological and physical health benefits to being a pet owner that can help alleviate depression.

Whenever people can take action to help others, they transcend their own negative feelings. Paradoxically, people who are depressed believe they need help rather than being aware that what they really need is to help others. It's a win–win situation. The depressed person feels better by moving outside his or her own zone of psychic pain and the recipient feels good about getting assistance.

Pause-and-Reflect Questions

1. Make a list of some of your own personal identifications. How do those identifications affect you?

2. Make a list of your positional identifications. How do those identifications affect you?

3. List one or more activities that you could provide to help others in need. Can you make a commitment to start that activity in the near future?

Belonging to a Group

Belonging to a group where there is a common interest is another way to combat depression. If you're like me, you may not be a joiner of groups. But here is one in which you might have an interest. The neurodiversity movement is an active group that many people with Asperger's have supported to improve the image of those on the autism spectrum. Those who support neurodiversity consider autism to be just a difference in brain functioning rather than a disease that requires a cure. The group's aim is to help educate the public to better understand, appreciate, and accept people who possess neurological differences from the mainstream population. Many people involved in this movement were despondent when they first learned of their Asperger's or autism diagnosis. They were lonely, depressed, and felt like second-class citizens. However, through the neurodiversity movement, they have a mutual goal that has linked them together in solidarity. Today, these same people that were once completely isolated are now actively participating in an important cause. In doing so, they have not only reduced their depression but have also helped others in the process.

It is fair to say that people with Asperger's don't have it easy in life. They face a myriad of daily challenges that most neurotypicals simply take for granted, including staying on top of household chores, keeping track of appointments, and having social interactions throughout the day with those they know as well as with strangers. Without realizing it, many of them are brave warriors who battle a multitude of obstacles and try to survive and make it to the end of each day. These struggles tend to begin at a very young age.

Life Challenges

Aspies usually experience their first psychological wounds as early as three or four years of age. These wounds begin to multiply exponentially as children grow up and are confronted with academic and social challenges. Being left out or rejected can often begin in a setting as seemingly benign as a mother–toddler group. Later on, students with Asperger's have to learn under the same teaching methodologies that are designed for neurotypicals. Often, these approaches produce ineffective and disappointing results.

Teachers frequently do not understand the behaviors of children with AS, such as their need to pace or their lack of attention to subjects in which they have no interest. Teachers are often critical of these behaviors, as opposed to understanding that these children have little control over them. Another issue of which teachers are frequently unaware is that children with AS need sufficient breaks between activities to cope with transitions. The net result of these educational missteps is that Aspies will often conclude that their academic problems reflect their lack of intelligence, and their potential for creativity will lie dormant. This sad state of affairs was even more prevalent for those who attended school prior to 1994, before the Asperger's diagnosis was identified in the *DSM-IV.*

Before that time, teachers had virtually no understanding of Asperger's and were unable to integrate children with AS in their classrooms. Teachers usually thought these children were lazy and weren't trying hard enough. I can remember my first-grade art teacher holding up one of my drawings and asking my fellow classmates, "Can you believe a first-grader did this?"

Besides teacher rejection, peers shunned these students for being eccentric, nonconformist, weird, and geeky. Who wouldn't be traumatized by being perceived so negatively by both teachers and classmates? In elementary school, I remember desperately wanting to fit in, but some of my behaviors were simply beyond my control. I had such an excess of energy that I would jump up and down and would often touch classmates on their heads. These odd behaviors were baffling to my teachers and peers, as well as to my parents.

I only had one teacher throughout elementary school who I felt made a genuine effort to get to know me. In third grade, I was lucky enough to have Kathy McCullough, a first-time teacher who was filled with enthusiasm and affection for her students. She was a huge change from my first and second-grade teachers who were both burned out from decades in the public school system. Ms. McCullough took a personal interest in me and was sensitive to my needs. She was aware of how much I liked tennis and actually made a date to play tennis with me over a weekend. I will never forget that day and what a lift it was to my spirits. Not only did we play a game of tennis at a park, but we also went to a restaurant for lunch. For the first time since starting elementary school, I felt accepted by a teacher. Other than Ms. McCullough, most teachers did not understand me. I usually came home from elementary school feeling slightly battered and depleted.

The need to conform and fit in with peers intensifies with puberty and becomes an almost impossible goal for children on the spectrum. Unlike the Buddha, who didn't become aware of imperfection until his adulthood, Aspies are introduced to their own imperfections early in life. Feeling inferior growing up is a strong predictor of adult depression. In order to gain more insight into what causes depression among Aspies, an examination of the theory of psychosocial development and the life cycle is needed.

Erikson's Theory of Psychosocial Development

In Erik Erikson's (1959) theory of psychosocial development, he presents a series of challenges, obstacles, and crises that exist at different stages of life. The goal of each stage is to overcome these obstacles and to successfully integrate the lessons learned before the next stage begins. When this takes place, one's personality becomes more adept at meeting future challenges that arise later in life.

In the first stage, which Erikson calls *trust versus mistrust*, the infant has to experience more trust than mistrust, but enough mistrust so that he learns that life isn't always predictable. Mothers don't always arrive the minute their infants cry out for food. Diapers aren't always changed as soon as they are soiled. The infant learns to adapt and to cope with some frustration that is internalized as a potential strength for dealing with circumstances in the future. The point is that if a baby didn't experience a sense of mistrust early in life, he would never become "immunized" to the feeling of not having his needs met later in life. In other words, he wouldn't be equipped to handle any frustration because it had never occurred earlier in his psychosocial development. The lessons to integrate in this first stage of development are that the world is a trustworthy place but not always predictable; frustration is inevitable but can be tolerated.

Each successful adaptation a child makes becomes more sophisticated and difficult than the one preceding it. According to Erikson, when the goals of a stage of development aren't met, the psychosocial development of the child can become arrested. For the purposes of this discussion, it is important to focus on the remaining stages of psychosocial developmental and how they relate to Asperger's and depression.

Stage two of Erikson's theory, *autonomy versus shame and doubt*, occurs in the toddler years during a child's first primitive taste of self-reliance. Unlike stage one, when an infant is totally dependent on his caregivers, toddlers are developing muscular control during stage two. They try to clap their hands, walk, hop, run, jump, and skip—skills that weren't possible in infancy. During this stage, toddlers also develop basic expressive and receptive language skills. Expressive language refers to what a child says. Receptive language refers to what a child comprehends.

Ideally in this stage, children begin moving away from their parents and interacting with other children their own age as well as with other adults such as babysitters, teachers, and extended family. If development in stage two proceeds normally, toddlers develop an insatiable appetite for independence tempered by the realization that only limited independence is possible. Parents optimally support the proper development of the child by providing opportunities to feel a safe amount of autonomy. What is commonly called the "terrible twos" refers to children taking ownership over everything they do and every choice they make, even if they have to say "no" or throw a tantrum in response to their commands. Being toilet-trained also furthers autonomy and a sense of mastery. If this stage of psychosocial development is not successfully achieved, a child can develop a sense of shame and doubt.

Many children on the spectrum have delayed language as toddlers (Attwood 2008) and are often unable to articulate what their minds want to express. I had a significant expressive and receptive speech delay as a toddler. I can actually remember the frustration I felt in knowing exactly what I wanted to say but not having the language skills to be able to say it. I also remember not being able to follow a directive that involved multiple steps, like "pick up the toy, put it in the box, and close the lid." I remember observing that other children my age could talk intelligibly, but I lacked the ability to express my thoughts in a similar fashion. This awareness of the difference in my language skills caused me to feel ashamed of myself and inferior to other children in social situations. When I was three years old, I received speech therapy three times a week at a local hospital. I had been diagnosed with a severe expressive and receptive language delay. However, after only a few months of intense therapy, my language skills were near age-appropriate levels. Despite the fact that I had caught up with my peers, I still continued to feel shame and self-doubt.

Unless we consciously deal with them, the feelings that get planted early in childhood will remain ever-present for the rest of our lives. A major factor contributing to low self-esteem and depression are the cognitive schemas—thoughts we have about ourselves—that are formed in early childhood, adolescence, and young adulthood that have not been adequately resolved.

The third stage that Erikson described is *initiative versus guilt* and begins at four or five years of age. At this stage the child is developing more neuromuscular control with respect to locomotion, meaning fine and gross motor skills. Typical tasks children master at this age include buttoning a shirt, zipping a jacket, tying shoes, cutting, pasting, and throwing and catching a ball. These tasks can be laborious for children who have difficulty with fine and gross motor skills. I know this from personal experience. I could not tie my shoes until I was ten, so I always wore shoes with Velcro. I stayed away from shirts with buttons until adolescence, and I avoided wearing belts. To this day, I have trouble knotting a tie.

If children have successfully developed the language and motor skills required in stage two, this mastery will lead to a sense of wanting to take the initiative in situations in stage three. They will say, "Pick me, pick me!" and, "I want to try, let me try!" At this stage, one's sense of identity is forming around the ability to make things happen at a very basic level, whether it is throwing and catching a ball, playing with others in a cooperative fashion, or trying to reach that cookie jar on top of the kitchen counter. Toys also provide an excellent outlet with which to experiment for children at this stage. They can take pride in their achievements and say, "Hey, I did that! I just blew that bubble!" "Wow. I moved my hand and the puppet talked. I can make things happen." The child has now developed a sense of purpose.

Another goal of stage three is appropriate socialization. Often peers reject children with Asperger's because they have trouble with simple games that involve coordination, or they can't express themselves at the same level as their classmates. A natural consequence of these developmental delays is that children with AS will perceive themselves as different from other children. In addition, they will experience shame that they are not getting the praise they see other children are receiving. Consequently, they may not take the initiative that would ordinarily be expected at this stage in the developmental sequence. Lack of confidence, guilt, and fear of rejection may develop at this early age and provide the underpinnings of future depression in adult life.

When I was in elementary school, my second grade teacher humiliated me in front of my classmates because I couldn't open the door to her room. In front of the other students in my class, Mrs. B. told me that a second-grader should be able to perform such a simple task. As she was delivering this diatribe, the children in the class were all laughing at me. I can remember feeling shame and embarrassment. I also felt that my peers were justified in ostracizing me. Many years later I came to realize I had carried this childhood trauma into my adulthood and would often feel incompetent and ashamed when I could not perform tasks that seemed easy for others to do. It is definitely worthwhile to examine how these types of early traumatic events can still be influencing one's present sense of self-esteem.

According to Erikson, if the objectives of stage three are not met, the child can feel a sense of guilt for not having the same muscular coordination as his peers. Perhaps, like me, he can't button his shirt or throw a ball, or is still having trouble with language acquisition. These types of tasks are difficult for children with Asperger's. Parents, caregivers, and teachers often become frustrated with these children after trying to work with them on these skills and seeing little progress.

The fourth stage of Eriksonian development begins around the time children enter first grade. Erikson called this stage *industry versus inferiority*. During this stage, children begin to establish a life for themselves outside of their parents' home. Though they are still under the close care, protection, and supervision of their parents, school represents a major change in their lives. All of a sudden, they are confronted with new demands imposed on them by the outside world. They must leave the comforts of home that offer a safe, secure, and predictable setting and enter a regimented environment known as school, where a multitude of transitions, social pressures, sensory irritations, and academic demands force them to adapt quickly to this new place. Unfortunately for the child with AS, adaptation to this strange, new, and confusing environment is rarely easy.

During this period of development, children are expected to be productive for the first time in their lives. In school, they are expected to behave well, get good grades, participate in after-school activities, and begin the process of successful socialization that will ideally form the foundation of friendship skills that will last a lifetime.

Children with Asperger syndrome struggle with these new expectations. If they don't behave well in school, they will be punished by their teachers, who are not always sympathetic to their differences. If they have trouble with certain academic tasks they will receive bad grades. They are forced to learn cursive handwriting and stay within the lines when coloring, even when they have poor fine motor skills, and they must also participate in physical education when gross motor skills may also not be a strong suit.

For all children, this is a particularly important developmental phase. For the child with AS, it becomes even more crucial, considering the formation of one's identity during these critical years. If the child struggles to fit in with a peer group and is viewed by teachers as lazy and noncompliant, he begins to feel different in a negative way from the rest of his classmates. He struggles to make it through each day without having a meltdown, and begins to develop a negative self-image.

In this stage, peers start to become as important, if not more so, than parents in a child's development. Children with Asperger's begin to experience significant problems in the area of socialization with peers. Their special interests often distance them from other children, and their difficulty in controlling their emotions is also a problem. Having outbursts, commonly referred to as meltdowns, is understandably viewed by peers as strange, inexplicable, and even scary. Further, they can often lead to bullying.

Sadly, teachers frequently lack sufficient knowledge of what learning style might bring out the best in this type of child. Even though the regimentation and structure of school *appears* to meet the needs of children with AS, the truth is this unpredictable environment causes the child much anxiety. A new bus driver, an unannounced school assembly, or any change in schedule can create stress and distract from the primary goals of education. The child with Asperger's begins to realize in elementary school that he does not fit in with either his peers or the educational program. These deficiencies can magnify feelings of inferiority.

The good news is that these negative feelings can be reversed. Throughout this book, I want to challenge the notion that nothing can be done to repair these early injuries to one's self-image. I want to provide knowledge and understanding to help heal the wounds of the past and the damage done to one's self-esteem.

Erikson's fifth stage of development is *identity versus role confusion.* This stage takes place during adolescence, when teenagers are immersed in a complex social milieu that is much more sophisticated than in previous stages. Keep in mind two general points about adolescence. First, every teenager, whether neurotypical or on the spectrum, experiences some role confusion during this stage. Second, adolescence is more extended now than it was in Erikson's day. People take more time to grow up now than in the past. This delay is why identity formation during the adolescent years may not be as crucial as it once was. Today, people stay in school longer, get married and have children later, and become completely independent at an older age than in previous generations.

Peer pressure to conform becomes the primary tool for achieving social success during this stage. Unusual, different, or quirky behavior is typically discouraged and rejected by peers. More advanced forms of nonverbal communication begin to emerge. Sarcasm and put-downs become part of the normal lexicon. Aspies will have difficulty in successfully engaging in social discourse because they lack the ability to interpret social cues. The essence of this stage is that teenagers, being on the crest of young adulthood, are beginning to break away from their parents and form a separate identity. In doing so, they attempt to merge their identity within a collective identity of their peers while also rebelling against societal expectations. This is often a time of great experimentation in which teenagers will try on many "hats" and change opinions on a regular basis regarding worldly, political, and spiritual concerns. In other words, teenagers are trying to find their place in the world.

Going from the fifth grade in elementary school to the sixth grade in middle school marks the beginning of the transition to adolescence. In fifth grade, students usually have only one assigned teacher and are with the same group of classmates throughout the entire day. Beginning in sixth grade, they attend different classes with different teachers. These changes are a lot to cope with in one year. Students also face a more demanding curriculum that requires increased hours spent doing homework. Greater organizational skills are needed to be able to meet these new educational demands. Peer pressure also has an impact on the collective mindset of adolescence. In essence, middle school is a whole new world.

As is typical for most children with Asperger's, middle school was an enormously difficult transition for me. I felt lost and adrift going from the relative security of elementary school into an enormous new building with different classrooms and teachers for each subject and a locker I could never keep clean or organized. After a couple of months, the guidance counselor called my parents in for a conference, telling them that she had never met a student who said he would rather be back in elementary school than in middle school.

Another problem I experienced was being in special education. Although I had received special education services from pre-kindergarten through fifth grade, it bothered me, but only a little. In middle school it was more apparent that I was a "sped," the term other kids used when talking about special education students. I began to hate special education and being different. I felt that way until I graduated from high school.

In this fifth stage, friendships with same-sex peers can become secondary to crushes or relationships with the opposite sex. If males have not started dating by the time they reach high school, they may start to feel unmanly. Others may think they are homosexuals. Flirting and the nuances of dating begin as early as middle school. Adolescents start to acquire the necessary practice and experience in dating that they will carry into young adulthood, when more serious and mature relationships begin to form.

What is this stage like for a teen with Asperger's, and more important, how might the effects of this stage lead to adult depression? During this tumultuous period of development, teens with AS will have an especially difficult time with friendships and dating because they are socially isolated and their sexual orientation may be questioned, adding to their role confusion. Adolescents who have not yet dated may begin to question their sexuality without realizing it is possible that their development is merely delayed rather than a function of their sexual orientation. Of course, there are some individuals on the autism spectrum who are gay, lesbian, bisexual, and transgender, and one can imagine the pain they might experience. In addition, there are others on the spectrum who struggle with their sexual orientation over a long period of time. I was one of those individuals who was confused about my sexuality because of my social isolation and lack of sexual experience, and it was only recently that I finally came to realize that I am gay.

Often parents tend to put pressure on their teenagers to socialize in conventional ways, like going to school dances, attending football games, and participating in after-school activities. Aspies who are forced to engage in these types of activities will feel high levels of personal discomfort. They look around and see their peers enjoying themselves and wonder why they don't feel the same way. They usually want to fit in, but realistically can only do so on their own terms. From a developmental point of view, not fitting in and being different will cement the sense of feeling like a perennial outsider. As one grows older and this pattern of isolation continues, it will reinforce feelings of shame and worthlessness and ultimately lead to depression.

The challenge of stage five is for adolescents to form an identity. Teens with Asperger's actually have a certain advantage during this stage of development. The literature is quite clear that they tend to be more immune to peer pressure than their neurotypical counterparts. Further, they seem to know what interests them irrespective of the approval of their peers.

This ability provides an irony to stage five. Theoretically, identity formation should be easier for those with Asperger's, but in reality, living in a neurotypical world frustrates their ability to derive positive feelings from their individuality. Therein lies the paradox. They lack acceptance from peers, teachers, and even parents and siblings, despite being more naturally capable than neurotypicals in identifying and pursuing their authentic needs and interests.

The character of Sheldon on the hit television show *The Big Bang Theory* embodies this description. A brilliant and eccentric scientist, Sheldon is keenly aware of his special interests and pursues them with relish, yet he seemingly could not care less about what anyone else thinks of him. However, not all Aspies are like Sheldon. Sadly, most people on the spectrum still want the approval of their peers or at least to create the illusion of fitting in.

Aspies can react to peer rejection in different ways. Some cover hurt feelings by displaying a grandiose attitude on the surface to hide feelings of insecurity and insignificance. Others withdraw into their own world, while a few become rebellious and act out against group norms and even authority figures.

If teens with AS could only know that life will get easier for them as they get older. When they become adults, they can look back and see that former peers who made fun of them were lacking in self-awareness or sensitivity. They would finally understand that those who bullied them years ago were the ones with the real personality disorder.

The sixth stage of psychosocial development is called *intimacy versus isolation* and takes place during young adulthood. This particular stage is especially challenging, but for Aspies it is what I would call the Olympics of Transition.

Typically, young neurotypical adults will engage in behaviors that will lead to them setting out on their own. If all goes according to plan, they will complete college, become romantically involved with a series of partners before getting married, and enter the workplace with the goal of becoming self-supporting. Unfortunately, Aspies encounter two major stumbling blocks during this period of time—difficulty with romantic relationships and problems gaining and maintaining employment. It is very easy to understand how failing to engage in these two very important adult activities would lead to depression. These two issues will be discussed in more detail in later chapters.

Chapter 2

Defining Depression

Having looked at the relationship between Asperger syndrome and depression, it is now important to understand why those on the spectrum are prone to depression. While the causes of depression are generally the same for neurotypicals as they are for those on the spectrum, there is a higher incidence of depression for those on the spectrum. Ghaziuddin (2005) reports that depression is the most common co-morbid (coexisting) mental condition that pervades the lifespan of an autistic person and notes that those on the high-functioning end of the autism spectrum seem to be particularly affected, which would clearly include those with Asperger syndrome. This corroborates other findings which suggest that those with a higher ability to evaluate their own social competence, or lack thereof, are more at risk of developing depression than those who lack this skill (Vickerstaff *et al.* 2006). Ghaziuddin and Greden (1998) also noticed that those with higher IQs on the spectrum tend to exhibit more depressive symptoms than those with lower IQs. The conclusion is that individuals with higher intelligence are better able to evaluate their level of social competence. Within that group, those who feel less socially competent are more likely to develop depressive symptoms.

Some global questions about depression are worth exploring: What are the factors contributing to depression? What are the different types of depression? Who is likely to be affected by depression? What are the different theories of depression? How can depression be managed, especially for people with Asperger's?

Life Transitions and Triggers

In looking back over my life, one factor always seems to be present prior to a depression and that is a *major life transition*. The following events all triggered episodes of depression of varying degrees:

- the transition from kindergarten to first grade

- the transition from elementary school to middle school

- the transition from high school to college

- the transition from college to the real world.

The literature is clear when it comes to the difficulties Aspies have with major life transitions. Stoddart (2005) notes that navigating the world as a fully autonomous person tends to be enormously challenging for individuals on the spectrum. He further states that:

> the developmental progression of a typical youth from adolescence to young adulthood can create major struggle for any family. The tensions in redefining parent–child boundaries and potentially competing roles of the parent and young adult can be confusing and challenging. Negotiating the rules of this period for young adults with AS is even more difficult because of the youth's exceptional needs and the lack of a clear understanding about how to address them. The shades of grey involved in the highly abstract and social transition to independence are difficult for the individual with AS to decipher. Such confusion for parents, for the young adult, and in community supports may be seen in disagreements about living arrangements, use of financial aid, post-secondary education

and career planning, management of mental health, motivation to accomplish goals, making friends and responses to the young adult's restricted range of interests. (Stoddart 2005, pp.85–86)

These developmental transformations occur as a natural part of the life cycle and may act as triggers for a depressive episode because people are especially vulnerable during these major life transitions. Certainly, life changes are among the most stressful events that people on the autism spectrum experience. Transitions are especially difficult for this group because they require adaptation, coping with change, shedding a part of one's identity and forming a new one, and loosening dependent ties with parents. The major difference between an Aspie's reaction to transitions and of some neurotypicals who psychologists would diagnose with an adjustment disorder is that Aspies typically have permanent challenges when dealing with change, as opposed to temporary ones.

Depression is fickle. What can trigger a depressive episode in one person might not even cause an emotional ripple in another. Everyone has unique triggers that can change over time. For one person, getting a flat tire can trigger a depression but for someone else, it might be the illness of a loved one. Since triggers can vary widely, one person's triggers may not make sense to others. Well-meaning friends and family will often try to convince someone that a particular trigger doesn't justify his being depressed. "A flat tire's no big thing. I can see being upset, but depressed? I don't get it." Each person has his own unique biochemistry that can create different responses to different situations.

Many factors can be at play in these varied responses. For example, the flat tire may have some psychological significance that interacts with low serotonin levels, thus creating a depression. Maybe that person doesn't know how to change a flat tire, which stimulates messages from childhood of being incompetent. Telling a friend not to get depressed by a particular trigger is like telling him not to say ouch when being given a shot.

On the other hand, we do not have to be victims of our triggers, whether they are biochemical or psychological. Through the use of antidepressants, psychotherapy, and other tools such as deep breathing, yoga, and meditation, people are finding ways to shift their brain chemistry and mind–body responses when confronted with triggers that have plagued them for years.

It is also helpful to become conscious of our triggers by writing them down and keeping track of them. A first step in that process would be to think about the times when life seemed to be smooth sailing, but then all of a sudden there was a dramatic mood shift.

For many years I was unaware that when I returned home from a vacation I would become depressed. The happy mood I had while I was on vacation turned fairly dark as soon as I came home. Many people experience a shift in mood upon returning from a trip but tend to bounce back in a day or two. That was not the case with me. Once I finally recognized that coming home from a trip was a trigger for depression, I was better prepared to deal with it. In being able to anticipate feeling sad, I would intentionally plan on doing something I enjoyed and could look forward to as soon as I got home. This planned activity gave me a sense of control and reduced or eliminated a depression upon my return.

Becoming aware of triggers can provide more knowledge to help ward off a depressive episode. There's nothing worse than getting hit with a bout of depression and not knowing where it comes from. Depression is bad enough without confusion or panic over its origin. Self-awareness makes it easier to spot patterns and trigger events that can forecast a possible dip into depression and to take active steps to cope with it.

A similar principle applies to paying attention to the factors contributing to a meltdown. Meltdowns do not usually occur out of the blue. Something or someone usually activates them. It is important to know what these triggers might be in order to take preventive measures either to eliminate the meltdown or mitigate its effects. This preventive approach is the same reason a person with diabetes carries a meter around with him and regularly tests his blood sugar. Someone who does a poor job of managing diabetes will frequently suffer from spells of low energy, hunger, thirst, or even nausea or fainting if not anticipating the triggers causing those conditions.

Aspies are known to have trouble dealing with sudden or unexpected changes in plans. Because these changes tend to occur spontaneously, they can't always be anticipated. However, there are certain times in which change is more likely to happen. Travel would be a good example. Plans often need to change due to a number of factors such as weather, health problems, and circumstances outside of one's control.

I remember the first time I drove from Detroit to Cleveland to visit my grandparents when I was 16. I was excited, but while driving on the turnpike, everything suddenly came to a screeching halt, and there was total gridlock. Later I found out there was an accident, but I didn't react very well. This was before cell phones, and I started to panic about arriving late. Knowing that travel can often create a change in plans, I am no longer as upset as I once was if something does not go according to plan. If an unexpected change is a trigger for you, perhaps there are things you can do to prepare yourself ahead of time. For example, if you have a flight delay, you might consider that possibility in advance, and bring along an absorbing book to read while you are waiting for your flight.

Regardless of the triggers, depression can wreak havoc on anyone's life regardless of race, socioeconomic status, religion, sexual orientation, or neurological wiring. Unfortunately, once one has had an episode of depression, one is likely to have further episodes (Mondimore 2006). However, the odds for relapse increase greatly for those who have never received any treatment for depression.

Pause-and-Reflect Questions

1. Can you identify any of your triggers for a depressive episode?

2. Once you are aware of your triggers, what can you do in anticipation of a depression or a meltdown?

How Depression Feels

Depression can cause the body to feel heavy, the muscles to feel sore, and the mind to feel numb. It can reduce its sufferers to nihilistic lumps of clay. When confronted with the daily chores of life, most depressed people simply retreat rather than try to confront their pain. They turn inward, looking for a safe place to hide, but find that only more pain awaits them. Both their interior and exterior worlds are inhospitable. This sad fate occurs when the outside world is viewed through a prism of negativity while the inner world is an emotional turmoil. Faced with what seems to be an uncaring, hostile environment, the depressed person seeks refuge by retreating, but his inner world is usually no less turbulent than the outer world. There is no place to run and no place to hide.

The great psychoanalyst Dr. Alexander Lowen (1972) once remarked that depression should not be equated with an emotion like sadness or "the blues." Many people believe that depression is akin to an intense feeling of sadness, like being grief-stricken when a loved one dies. It might be surprising to learn that depression isn't really an emotion, like sadness, jealousy or anger. On the contrary, many experts define depression as the absence of emotion, an emotional void where one feels numb. When people are depressed, they feel lifeless and have no energy. A fancy term for this state is *psychomotor retardation*, which refers to the fact that depression seems to put the body into somewhat of a vegetative state. Some severely depressed people find simple acts like walking their dog or combing their hair to be arduous chores. In *The Noonday Demon*, author Andrew Solomon (2001) remarked that when he was in the depths of a depressive episode, he had to be spoon-fed by his father. He literally didn't have the energy to manipulate the silverware to scoop up the food and bring it to his mouth. In her book *Shoot the Damn Dog* (2008), Sally Brampton confessed that when her depression struck, she couldn't even leave her bedroom. She described her emotional state as a kind of "punished helplessness" and she experienced a complete disintegration of everything she had ever known about herself. Brampton no longer had control over anything in her life including her thoughts, emotions, her appetite, and her ability to sleep.

Some people also experience very unpleasant physical symptoms associated with their depression. In John Bentley Mays' *In the Jaws of the Black Dogs: A Memoir of Depression* (1999), he wrote that his depression began with sharp, knife-like pains. Soon after, he would have severe abdominal cramping and intense diarrhea. He was so lacking in energy that he wasn't even able to go and see a doctor.

A few years ago I was suffering with flu-like symptoms. I had a fever and a sore throat and felt completely exhausted. The symptoms got worse, and it took a few weeks before I was diagnosed with mononucleosis. This illness mirrored the depression I was experiencing at the time to such an extent that I almost could not distinguish between the two ailments. Mono, like depression, robs one of energy. Both conditions muddy one's thought processes, disrupt cognition, slow down neuromuscular reaction time, and, in general, make one feel horrible. Initially I thought my lethargy was just another depressive episode, but when the illness progressed to the point where my fever was 103 degrees, it finally became clear that what I had was a virus caused by an outside agent, rather than a virus from within.

I intentionally used the phrase "virus from within" because depression can feel as though something foreign is attacking the body. Not only can depression separate you from yourself, if it lingers too long, as it did with Sally Brampton, you can lose your sense of self. In the worst-case scenarios, depression can take over your entire identity. Once you've reached the stage where you have difficulty remembering what life was like before becoming depressed, the goal in treatment would be to help reclaim your "essential self," also known as the human spirit.

Depression is so powerful it can destroy the essential self. I know this from firsthand experience. Although I had some social and educational problems in elementary school, I was a very happy child at home. However, when I entered middle school, there was a dramatic shift in my entire being. In elementary school I was generally in a good mood and had a couple of friends. I had a smile on my face and radiated an energy that was contagious. I was funny and outgoing. When I look at home movies of myself at that age, I can hardly believe what I see. I was a joyful little boy who loved life and was excited about everything around him. But almost as soon as I started middle school, this zest for life vanished and the onset of depression completely took over.

During the first year of middle school I started to feel that parts of myself were disappearing and I was becoming a shadow of my former self. In elementary school I had definite interests and enjoyed pursuing them. I liked to listen to oldies music and watch television game shows. *The Price is Right, Card Sharks,* and *Wheel of Fortune* were some of my favorites. People often commented to my parents about my enthusiastic spirit. In middle school all that changed. I was embarrassed that other kids didn't like what I liked, so I pretended to like what they did. My energy decreased, I rarely smiled, and I became very isolated.

On some days, my dad would drive me and some other kids in my neighborhood to school. I would always switch the radio station from what I usually listened to (oldies) to the hard rock station. I didn't want the other kids to know the kind of music I liked.

How did I go from a being happy to depressed in such a short period of time? Looking back on it, I think there was a confluence of factors that created the perfect storm that year. Among the factors were social isolation, bullying at school, an educational system that did not respond to the bullying, and teachers who did not understand my differences. This combination of issues threw me into an emotional tailspin from which it took years to recover.

Metaphorically speaking, entering sixth grade was the year I "left the palace." Like Siddhartha, I left my very protected home and elementary school and entered the harsher environment of middle school. The sense I had of being protected was gone. I no longer felt innocent. The world as I knew it had changed dramatically, and I began to attune myself both to my own suffering as well as that of others. In hindsight, it makes sense that I became depressed at this time.

Since that first bout of sadness in middle school, I've learned a lot about managing episodes of depression. Fortunately, I've matured a lot over the years. I've also become a lot more self-aware and have tried a number of treatments that have been extremely successful. I will share these treatments in later chapters.

The Inner Critic

Depression numbs one to the external world as well as turning the psyche against itself, much like a mental autoimmune disorder. In Freudian terms, the superego, or "inner critic" (the judgmental part of one's personality) persuades a person that he is worthless and, in extreme cases, not entitled to live. Depression can transform the smartest and toughest people into self-loathing individuals. It is hard to imagine that rugged men like Mike Wallace, the former *Sixty Minutes* correspondent, and William Styron, the noted author, suffered so deeply with depression that at times they were both suicidal. Both men wrote books about their battles with depression and talked about how those close to them often felt helpless watching them change from vibrant, active people to zombies who felt no joy in living. Styron's depression didn't happen until his sixties. In *Darkness Visible* (1990), his short but powerful book, he detailed how depression came close to destroying his spirit.

In an effort to shield themselves from a constantly disappointing world as well as the voice of their abusive inner critic, depressed people unconsciously shut down all their feelings. Their rationale is that feeling nothing is better than feeling pain. Just as the body's immune system fights physical disease, the mind tries to fight pain by eliminating feelings and thereby anesthetizing oneself to life. Depressed people may stop listening to music because it evokes specific emotions. They might forgo taking trips because their inner critic says they don't deserve a positive experience. They may give up exercising because it takes too much energy.

Drug and alcohol abuse are often the most common choices for distancing oneself from feelings. Another option is sleep. Excessive sleeping is one of the hallmarks of depression. Insomnia, its opposite, can also be a symptom. For me, sleep is always a good indicator of where I stand with depression. If I am sleeping fairly regularly, that is a sign I am in a good place. If I am sleeping more than nine hours a night or not being able to fall asleep or stay asleep for several days in a row, that is a warning sign.

Shutting down one's feelings in the extreme is described by autism author Donna Williams in her book *Nobody Nowhere: The Extraordinary Autobiography of an Autistic* (1999). "Exposure anxiety" (Williams 2002) is the term she coined to describe a self-protective mechanism that shields one from the outside world. In Williams's framing of this term, exposure anxiety is like an internal parent who watches over and protects her infant. This inner parent provides a sanctuary that will shield her child from an over-stimulating, terrifying world. However, the result of this hyper-vigilance is that the child ends up feeling suffocated. Although the intention of this internal parent is to protect against sensory and emotional flooding, Williams said it created for her "a big black hole of nothingness" (2002, p.71) where she virtually lost connection to her outer reality. As a toddler she fell into the "big black hole" (p.71) as often as six times a day. As she grew older she shielded herself from everyone so that they wouldn't provoke any emotion in her. This self-protective mechanism may have served her well in childhood, but not as an adult.

The term *internalized homophobia* describes a self-protective mechanism that gays use to internalize negative societal attitudes regarding homosexuality. This mechanism takes effect when gays identify with the pejorative messages they have received about homosexuality since childhood. These negative messages may have come from church leaders, politicians who are against gay marriage, school bullies, or comedians who make fun of homosexuals. What often happens is the gay person absorbs the homophobia that permeates society. Psychotherapists well versed in issues involving the gay community are quite familiar with how this process operates and, in fact, anticipate it as an obstacle toward self-acceptance and positive change. A good example of internalized homophobia are closeted politicians who engage in anti-gay rhetoric while experiencing self-hatred. I experienced this same kind of self-hatred by absorbing society's negative attitudes regarding homosexuality. I was constantly hearing negative comments about being gay from the media, my classmates, and even one of my athletic coaches. I concluded that being gay was something I never wanted to be.

Just as a segment of gays have internalized negative messages about homosexuality, many on the spectrum have accepted as true pejorative statements about people with autism. One might call this phenomenon internalized autiephobia (where "autie" is the autistic equivalent of an Aspie) or internalized Aspiephobia. Besides what they have heard or read in the media, those on the spectrum have also personally received negative messages about certain autistic traits over which they have no control. Teachers may have reprimanded them for being disorganized, stupid, or not trying to succeed. Peers may not have wanted them to be on their teams in gym class because they were uncoordinated. Bullies may have teased them for being weird in some way, and parents might have yelled at them for acting crazy when they were having a meltdown. Many on the spectrum internalize those messages.

The one difference between Asperger syndrome and depression is that almost everyone agrees depression should be treated, managed, or cured. In contrast, not everyone believes that Asperger syndrome should be similarly approached. I believe the deep-rooted shame of internalized Aspiephobia often prevents individuals with Asperger's from being able to accept their strengths and to maximize their true potential.

Internalizing negative messages about oneself can continue into adulthood. The inner critic, especially for people with Asperger's, may be harsh in making judgments about issues regarding employment and romance, two major life issues. Many people struggle to stay employed, but for those with Asperger's it is doubly challenging. They often have to function in a fast-paced, high-pressured workplace where their individual strengths, like the ability to focus, honesty, and dependability, are not always appreciated. In addition, they also lack the social skills to form and maintain relationships on the job. Some neurotypicals may be shier than others but do not have the same level of anxiety and discomfort as those with Asperger's.

Negative messages like, "You're such a geek" and "Why don't you have a girlfriend like everyone else?" fuel the inner critic. It takes a lot of effort to pay attention to these thoughts that reflect critical self-judgment. But if you do, you will eventually realize your inner critic sounds a lot like the people who are critical of you.

Another term for internalizing negative judgments is the *delusion of moral inferiority*, first articulated by psychoanalyst Sandor Rado (Gaylin 1983). Rado explains that people with depression are usually too dependent on the judgments of others for their own sense of self-esteem. In the case of someone with Asperger's, it's easy to see how this might be true. Remember the discussion of Erikson's theory of psychosocial development in Chapter 1? In these early stages of life, from childhood to adolescence through young adulthood, individuals with Asperger's are frequently scorned for simply being themselves. They were told their meltdowns were unacceptable, their interests were strange, and they weren't trying hard enough to make friends or to do well in school. Because they were not validated for who they were, they naturally invalidated themselves.

Imagine how it would feel if no one acknowledged your presence for a week. On the first day, you approach a group of people standing by the water cooler at work, but no one looks at you. Then the next day, you try asking for help at an electronics store, but none of the salespeople seem to notice you. By the third day, you would probably be begging people to acknowledge your presence and be projecting a neediness that could provoke negative reactions. At the end of a week of having had a number of these experiences, how do you think you would you feel? Probably like you didn't exist.

When people experience an inordinate amount of rejection and isolation, they feel invisible. The self internalizes these feelings of rejection, integrates them into consciousness and then uses them as a protective mechanism to deflect the hurtful conduct of others. The paradox is that while the depressed person needs more validation to sustain a healthy sense of self than most others, the depressed person's inner critic will usually reject any kind of positive feedback as being untrue.

People on the spectrum often have a hard time accepting a compliment. They will either reject it outright or their inner critic will find a reason to refute it. Sometimes after I gave a presentation, audience members will tell me how much they enjoyed my speech. Rather than accept the compliment, I might respond, "Thanks, but it wasn't one of my better speeches." Alternatively, my inner critic will whisper in my ear, "He's just saying that to make you feel good. He doesn't really mean it." It's like saying to someone at the dinner table, "Please pass the peas," and once the peas are within reach, pushing them away.

Heinz Kohut (Siegal 1996), a psychoanalyst and the founder of self-psychology, states that the self is primarily defined through the lens of interpersonal relationships. In other words, my sense of self grows stronger the more people who affirm me, believe in my potential, and give me proper support and encouragement. Conversely, I begin to form a more negative picture about myself if none of these connections with others have occurred. In essence, we need positive feedback from others in order to thrive.

Growing up, I was an excellent tennis player and wanted to be on my high school team. I not only wanted to be on the team, but I also wanted to play number one singles. The coach was very tough and told everyone they would "have to work their butts off" to make the team. I started to have doubts about my ability, and I wasn't performing well in the tryouts. At first the coach gave me very little feedback about how I was doing. This lack of feedback only made me feel more insecure, but after about a week, he told me he thought that my strokes were solid and that I could be good enough to play number one singles. That conversation produced an immediate change in my self-image. Suddenly, I believed I could succeed and achieve my goal. My tennis game hadn't changed that much. What had changed was my coach had encouraged me and said he believed in me. Therefore, I started to believe in myself.

Positive feedback, an essential source of self-esteem, is often absent for those with Asperger's. I grew up at a time when the diagnosis did not yet exist, and the educational system was clueless about kids with AS. Parents of Aspies were also perplexed by their children's unusual or quirky behaviors and often tried to make their children behave more conventionally, which was often contrary to their neurological wiring. Because there was no paradigm for

Asperger syndrome at the time, I, along with many others, was not successful in school and felt like a visitor from another planet. Although educators have made progress in the last 20 years, most employers have not. Employers are as mystified about people with Asperger's as educators were two decades ago. One can see why so many smart, creative, and highly qualified Aspies aren't making strides in the workplace. If employers had the same information that today's educators now have, they would become more aware of the inherent strengths that Aspies possess and view them as valued employees.

Sigmund Freud theorized that depression is anger turned inward. In other words, feeling prolonged anger at oneself fuels the energy of depression. Many on the autism spectrum epitomize that theory. Given their years of mistreatment by others, they have accumulated a storehouse of anger they have turned on themselves. However, the resulting depression does not have to be a permanent condition.

All feelings have cycles. Like a weather system, no emotion lasts forever. Even pain naturally abates. As a child, when you skinned your knee, you learned Mommy would treat and kiss the wound, and pretty soon everything would be all better. In an emotionally healthy person, feelings are fluid and are always subject to change, but a depressed person loses that sense of fluidity and becomes convinced that the condition is permanent. It is as if the mind needs to shut down because a foreign invader has attacked its normal functioning, much like a virus that invades a computer. In a depressed state, one is convinced that the current feeling will remain that way forever.

Certain people may always struggle with depression but it does not have to ruin the quality of their lives. A person with diabetes can live to a ripe old age if he takes proper care of the disease. Even someone with the HIV virus can live a meaningful life with appropriate medication. Depression may always be lurking in a person's mental landscape, but it can be successfully managed.

When you experience depression, the most effective antidote is to be compassionate and loving toward yourself. Unconditional love is not just for other people. Through the use of cognitive distortions (negative ways of thinking) the inner critic will take the opportunity to destroy any positive feedback others give you as well as any positive affirmations you may give yourself. I spent a great deal of time talking about cognitive distortions in my previous book, *Asperger Syndrome and Anxiety* (2009), and received a positive response to my discussion of cognitive–behavioral therapy. The next chapter of this book will be devoted to the subject.

Unfortunately, cognitive distortions play an even greater role in depression than with anxiety because the job of the inner critic is to make you feel bad about yourself. The temptation is either to try to block out that critic or to overly indulge it. Either way leads to low self-esteem, the hallmark of depression.

Pause-and-Reflect Questions

1. On a scale of 1 to 10 (with 10 being the highest), how tough is your inner critic?

2. In what ways have you tried to silence your inner critic?

3. What are some of the criticisms from others you have internalized about yourself?

Learned Helplessness

Have you ever noticed that when you are depressed, almost any task seems excruciatingly difficult to do? "Learned helplessness," the well-known model proposed by psychologist Martin Seligman, explains this type of observation in many depressed people. Seligman discovered when restrained dogs were given strong electric shocks, they had more difficulty learning how to escape once their restraints were removed than the dogs who received more moderate shocks (Papolos and Papolos 1997). One conclusion that can be drawn from this study is the dogs that received the more severe shocks were conditioned by their external environment to believe they had no ability to escape at all. This experiment demonstrated that the dogs had learned from their environment to be helpless. Seligman's research demonstrated that this model of behavior is also true for humans.

A study by Ozment and Lester (1998) demonstrated a strong correlation between learned helplessness and depression among 70 undergraduate college students. Learned helplessness takes place when life's stresses impinge on one's sense of competency and affect the locus of control, which is the extent to which people feel control over a situation. For example, if I were to play a tennis match against someone who was not as skilled as me, my locus of control would be quite high. I would have to play poorly in order to lose. The outcome of the match would rest more on the quality of my game rather than on any other factor. Conversely, if I had to play Roger Federer, one of the best tennis players of all time, my locus of control would be extremely low. Federer would have to come to the court with two broken legs in order for me to have any chance to win. The outcome of the game would not rest with my locus of control, but with his inability to play as he normally would.

Similarly, the way in which people think about past successes or failures will have an impact on their level of self-esteem and locus of control. Depressed people tend to imbue negative past events with the ability to continue to have a negative impact into the future. These negative experiences become global and take on more significance than the event itself and morph into a generalized thought. Also, depressed people tend to blame themselves for these negative experiences, whereas those who aren't depressed generally consider them to be isolated with no particular significance for the future (Kambara and Sakamoto 1998).

If I had a couple of bad meals the last few times I went out to eat at a restaurant, I could turn that into a global statement: eating in restaurants is bad. I could further blame myself and make another global statement: I always order the wrong thing when I go out to eat.

A true or factual global statement would be: everyone breathes oxygen. A global statement is stable over time and means that things will remain the way they are indefinitely. Another global statement would be: gravity causes a ball that is thrown up in the air to always fall back to the ground. Whereas these two examples are factually true, global statements that arise from negative personal experiences are often unexamined and false.

The term "internally caused" describes a situation where a person who has a negative experience blames himself, rather than attributing it to happenstance or chance. For example, the statement "I always order the wrong thing" expresses a generalized pessimistic viewpoint. This statement is global in nature because the content is expressed as a fact that describes one's being in the same way in which one might state a physical characteristic like height or eye color. This stated belief also applies into the future and connotes the inability to ever achieve a positive outcome.

In contrast, a non-depressed person will usually attribute negative events to random and unpredictable causes. Instead of blaming myself for always ordering the wrong thing, I would assume that what I had previously ordered was just bad luck and would order something different the next time. No generalization would flow from my bad experiences.

Another example of blaming oneself for external circumstances would be if my boss was in a bad mood and yelled at me for no apparent reason. Rather than assume this outburst was because of something I did, I might consider the fact that he is going through a divorce and displacing his frustration on me. In doing so, I would not be taking responsibility for causing his behavior.

This is not to suggest that people should never take responsibility for negative experiences, but realizing your boss may be in a bad mood for reasons not connected to you may be a more accurate way of assessing the situation than automatically assuming you are to blame. Try to become more conscious and analyze the link between your inner critic's global statements about yourself and your depression. If you believe nothing ever turns out well because of your inherent flaws, you may have stopped expecting to ever have a positive experience. Had I adopted that negative global mindset, I might not have ever become a successful athlete in high school and college.

THE AUTISM SPECTRUM AND DEPRESSION

As I mentioned earlier, I am five feet, six inches tall. Despite my height, I was a championship tennis player in high school and college. I had to play some very tall opponents who had certain physical advantages over me. When I played basketball in middle school—somewhat unsuccessfully because I am short—I didn't globalize that my height would keep me from competing in *all* sports. Although I had a disadvantage in tennis against taller opponents, there were other skills I could still use to be successful. Because I was open to the possibility of doing well in sports other than basketball, I was able to proceed and become an all-state tennis player and was ranked number one in Southeastern Michigan. Had I formed a generalized statement about my height, I would have felt hopeless about participating in any sport.

A sense of hopelessness is the cornerstone of depression. Like the dogs that learn it is impossible to escape even when they are no longer being shocked or in restraints, Aspies learn to feel hopeless that things in their lives—school, friendships, and employment—will ever go well. Recently I had a conversation with an 18-year-old who was convinced that as long as he had Asperger syndrome, he would never have a sexual experience. He attributed his inability to have sex to having Asperger's and said that unless he was somehow "cured," he would never have sex during his life. When I attempted to point out that many people, especially those on the spectrum, don't lose their virginity until well past their teens, it made no difference to him. He felt hopeless about his chances to have sex and this belief made him despair.

I personally understand why this young man viewed the odds of having sex to be so slim. Most Aspies, including myself, find any type of socializing to be challenging, but a person's beliefs will have a serious impact upon his sense of control. Remember, a lack of control fuels depression. Attributing negative past experiences and future outcomes to undesirable traits only leads to self-loathing.

I encouraged readers in *Asperger Syndrome and Anxiety* (2009) to think of themselves as brave warriors going into battle. The willingness to participate in life's daily activities often requires acts of bravery, such as dealing with salespeople, socializing with co-workers, and going through difficult transitions. Confronting all these stressors in just one day can be intimidating for those on the spectrum.

Again, like the dogs Seligman described in his theory of learned helplessness, those on the spectrum may receive a metaphoric shock every time they try to ask someone on a date, mingle at a party, or apply for a job. These shocks bring up past negative experiences that in reality do not necessarily predict future outcomes. Unfortunately, receiving all these shocks in early childhood may cause people with Asperger's not to try to achieve their goals.

Instead of being judged by the standards of others that are difficult or impossible to meet, those with Asperger's need to set their own learning curve. That doesn't mean giving up on what most people want out of life, but rather not expecting to be as initially proficient in certain areas as neurotypicals. Aspies are usually late bloomers. Just as they receive extended time to complete tests in school, they sometimes need extra time to develop certain skills. If someone criticizes you according to neurotypical standards, that is his problem. What matters is what you think of yourself. Getting your inner critic to relax a little will make you feel less helpless and more in control of achieving success.

Every night I like to review the challenges of my day and acknowledge triumphs, both large and small. It is important not to be critical in this process or judge yourself by other people's standards. Accomplishing something that is difficult for you but easy for someone else should not diminish the pride you take in that achievement.

For instance, if I have to return an item I bought at the hardware store that is not working properly, I might tell myself that even though it is not functioning properly, it will be too stressful for me to have to return it. I might also feel ashamed that other people would have no problem returning the item. Instead of engaging in these negative thoughts, I need to be able to return the item and then celebrate the fact that I was able to do it and get my money back. It might seem silly to acknowledge these small victories, but the only person you can compare yourself to is you.

Many years ago, when I imagined what my life would be like as an adult, I envisioned being married and having children. When I finally came to the realization that I would probably need most of my energy to take care of myself, I had to conclude that I might not have a family. Disengaging from that vision was not easy for me. The acceptance of that reality required me to refocus my goals to fit more accurately my needs and not necessarily those of mainstream society. Comparisons to others are always fruitless, whether a person is on the spectrum or not. Self-acceptance and pride in your individuality mitigates the helplessness that underlies depression and allows you to lead your life on your own terms.

The Science of Depression

To understand the biological causes of depression, it is necessary to learn a little bit about how neurons and neurotransmitters work. Neurons are cells within the brain and spinal cord that communicate with each other through electrical and chemical processes. We have many different types of neurons that serve a multitude of purposes, but the most important point to remember is that a neuron communicates with other neurons through a neurotransmitter that is a chemical messenger in the brain. The neurons do not actually touch each other but instead engage in a process called *synaptic transmission*. When one neuron wants to communicate with another neuron, it must dump its neurotransmitters into a tiny gap called a synapse, hoping the next neuron will receive the message. The presynaptic neuron (the neuron doing the dumping) receives a shot of calcium at the end of the neuron called the axon terminal. This causes an action potential, wherein the presynaptic neuron dumps the neurotransmitters in the synaptic cleft, which is the tiny gap. Once the neurotransmitters are in the synapse, one of three things usually happens. The postsynaptic neuron's protein receptor binds to the neurotransmitters in the synapse and they are absorbed through the dendrites of that neuron; or they are disposed of; or they are reabsorbed back into the presynaptic neuron. Each presynaptic neuron has the potential to influence the postsynaptic neuron, which, in turn, can influence the next one down the line, followed by the next, and so on. So why is all this scientific information relevant to the discussion of depression?

Three neurotransmitters have been found to be particularly important to the study of depression. They are norepinephrine, serotonin, and dopamine. Since the 1960s, research has shown that decreased levels of norepinephrine cause sluggishness, reduced libido, inattentiveness, and depression. Serotonin is known as the mood stabilizer (Cousens 2000). Low levels of serotonin have been linked to depression, cravings for carbohydrates, aggression, violence, and suicide. Serotonin is synthesized from tryptophan and 5-hydroxytryptophan (5HTP). Foods such as eggs, soy-based products, red meat, and anything with protein contain tryptophan. Vitamin B6 can help with the conversion of tryptophan to serotonin. Low B6 levels may indicate a serotonin deficiency, which can cause depression. Drinking alcohol is one way to deplete vitamin B6 levels.

If serotonin is a mood stabilizer, then dopamine is a mood elevator that can bring pleasure. What can increase dopamine? Receiving a compliment. Having sex. Eating chocolate. Playing a sport. In other words, interacting with or even observing stimuli that one finds appealing. Lack of dopamine tends to be implicated with depression and Parkinson's disease, but too much dopamine can create heightened states like mania as well as schizophrenia. Wheat germ is a good source of phenylalanine, which is the raw material from which dopamine is synthesized.

Certain antidepressants have been designed to stop the reuptake (or reabsorbing) of the serotonin and norepinephrine back into the presynaptic neuron. The goal of these drugs is to help with the transfer of the neurotransmitters within the synapse from the presynaptic to the postsynaptic neuron by preventing reuptake from happening or at least decreasing it significantly. These are called selective serotonin reuptake inhibitors (SSRIs). Many people who take antidepressants experience some relief from the distressing symptoms of depression. However, medication alone doesn't cure depression, and medication should only be taken under the close supervision of a primary care physician or psychiatrist.

Some research has suggested that people with Asperger syndrome have low serotonin levels. One study in 2006 found that individuals with Asperger's had significantly reduced 5HTP receptors. This means they had reduced "serotonergic responsivity" (Murphy *et al.* 2006). Additionally, low levels of tryptophan have been documented in autistic children, which suggests that the conversion of tryptophan to serotonin may be lacking. Physicians can order tests to measure these levels.

Vitamin D can play a role in causing depression if one's levels are too low. People in the Northern Hemisphere (especially those in the middle and eastern parts of the United States, as well as northern countries and places near the Arctic Circle) are more vulnerable to lack of sunlight in the winter months. The sun is the main source from which we derive vitamin D. It is produced on the skin after spending at least 20 to 30 minutes in the sunlight on a daily basis (Cousens 2000). It has been shown that the sensory defensiveness that those on the spectrum experience (e.g. aversion to the bright light of the sun, traffic noise, etc.) may cause many of them to spend less time in the sun than their neurotypical counterparts. (On the other hand, many people on the spectrum love to spend time outside with nature where it is quiet.)

Everyone should make sure they have enough vitamin D in their diet or, with a doctor's supervision, take a multivitamin or vitamin D supplement. Recently, I had a physical examination and found out that I was deficient in vitamin D and am now taking a supplement. Foods like eggs, cheese, and salmon contain vitamin D, but again, the best source comes from the sun.

The importance of a good night's sleep in managing depression is critical. Disturbances in one's circadian rhythms also play a role in mood-related disorders such as depression (Germain and Kupfer 2008). Circadian rhythms govern the sleep–wake cycle and exist in everything from bacteria to human beings. An inability to fall asleep is generally a symptom with most types of depression, excluding atypical depression. Almost everyone I've met with Asperger's has told me about problems falling asleep at night or getting back to sleep if awakened in the middle of the night. Some research has indicated that children with Asperger's have problems with daytime sleepiness, sleep duration, waking up too early in the morning, and restless sleep (Bruni *et al.* 2007). Later I will return to this subject and offer some suggestions on ways to get a better night's sleep.

Genetics also plays a role in who might be more susceptible to depression. Studies reveal that an identical twin (who has the same exact genes as their twin) of a person with depression is much more prone to developing depression than a fraternal twin (who has only half their genes in common). Similarly, children of parents who are depressed are more genetically at risk for depression than adopted children of depressed parents. Finally, those with a short version of a certain gene known as the serotonin transporter are two-and-a-half times more likely to become depressed when faced with the same stressful, negative events as others without that gene.

Apart from biological causes, there are also many studies that suggest early childhood trauma contributes to adult depression. Charles Whitfield, the author of *Healing the Child Within* (1987) and *The Truth about Depression* (2003), who admittedly has a bias against biological factors of depression, analyzed 70 studies involving almost 70,000 victims of childhood trauma and found that suicidality increased by 10 to 18 times from that of the control group. Whitfield (2003) also found an additional 96 other studies from 1942 to 2003 showing the same to be true with over 29,000 subjects when compared with controls. There is no doubt that childhood trauma can and does play a role in manifesting depression in adulthood. The relevance of that statement for those with Asperger's becomes very significant when considering that most Aspies have been bullied, misunderstood, or scorned for their differences as children.

Types of Depression

Prolonged depression usually produces devastating consequences, but not every form of depression is the same. Treatment plans vary depending upon the type of depression a person has. Like most things in life, depression is on a spectrum. A person with a major depressive disorder behaves a lot differently than someone suffering from dysthymia, a chronic but less severe form of depression. Therefore, it's important to distinguish between the various types of depression.

I met Kim (not her real name) several years ago. She was an extremely intelligent woman who was diagnosed with Asperger's in her 30s. Kim was functioning well. She was going to work, attending an Asperger's support group, and occasionally getting together with friends. However, I couldn't help but notice that Kim looked sad much of the time. She barely smiled, didn't seem happy about anything in her life, and preferred to keep a low profile. Kim told me she felt like everything in her life was tinged with sorrow. She said food tasted blander than normal, her relationships were strained, and she didn't have enough energy to exercise. Shortly after our conversation, Kim was diagnosed with dysthymia, a low-grade type of depression.

A dysthymic individual is not a person who can't get out of bed in the morning and barely makes it to the shower. The symptoms of major depression are still there but with far less intensity. With dysthymia, a person still suffers from low self-esteem, low energy, irritability, and all the other characteristics of depression. Dysthymia is often classified as a chronic mood disorder that must be present for at least two years before it can be diagnosed. According to the *DSM-IV* (used by the American Psychological Association), a person must have experienced the following criteria for a period of two years:

- a poor appetite or overeating
- difficulty sleeping or too much sleep
- low energy or fatigue
- low self-esteem
- poor concentration or difficulty making decisions
- feelings of hopelessness.

If a major depression occurs during this two-year period, a diagnosis of dysthymia cannot be made. However, this type of long-term, low-grade depression brings with it a greater risk of a major depressive episode in the future. After two years have passed and a major depressive episode does occur, it is called a double depression.

Since dysthymia is milder than a major depression, friends and family may not understand the nature of the disorder or be empathic to someone who is suffering from it. Those with dysthymia will often try to act as if nothing is bothering them and everything is just fine. This pressure to act normally sounds like someone with Asperger's trying to behave as neurotypically as possible. Another feature these two conditions have in common is that just as an Aspie can be criticized for being eccentric, disruptive, and rigid, sufferers of dysthymia can be accused of being moody, sulky, or having a bad attitude. It goes without saying that such misguided criticism is not helpful.

A common subtype of dysthymia is atypical depression. Those with atypical depression will usually respond positively to enjoyable events and personal compliments, unlike those who suffer from depression. Atypical depression is also characterized by reversed vegetative symptoms, meaning the person tends to overeat and oversleep. It is often referred to as a "reactive depression" or a "situational depression" because one's mood is generally affected by both positive and negative reinforcements from the environment.

I am not implying that atypical depression is better than "regular" depression. It's just different. Obviously people with atypical depression are more prone to positive moods if good things are happening to them, but they are equally affected by negative circumstances. To the extent that someone can actually experience joy when things are going well, the atypical subtype has more functionality in life.

However, atypical depression has one major drawback. Happiness depends solely on external circumstances. Atypical depression is something like having little sugar rushes from time to time. When you eat sugar, you experience a high for a short period of time but after a while, you crash and start craving more sugar. Being dependent on other people's approval or needing to have good things happen to you in order to be happy is like eating sugar. No one, not even the most fortunate among us, goes through life without his or her share of hard times and disapproval. The positive feelings won't last very long before someone rejects you or something goes wrong.

Another term for this cycle of pursuing pleasure and then crashing is the "if only" syndrome. If only I get a girlfriend, my life will be complete. If only I would win the lottery, life would be great. If only (fill in the blank), I'll be happy. But of course, there is always another "if only."

Those with atypical depression also have a low locus of control because their happiness rests on people and events outside of themselves. They defer approval to others instead of relying on their own judgment. They generally feel powerless victims of life's circumstances. The treatment goal for someone with this diagnosis would be to help establish a baseline level of happiness commensurate with one's self-worth so the external circumstances of life don't dictate the fluctuations of happiness and sadness as much.

Depression can take a more philosophical form called *ontological rejection*. This type of depression is when one views other people as inherently selfish and the basic nature of the universe as unjust or misguided. This broad rejection of the creation of all matter reflects contempt for how the universe is run and often results in anger toward or total rejection of God. This belief doesn't mean depressed people are atheists. Most atheists are untroubled by not believing in a benevolent supernatural force at work. They feel that the beauty of life is more in the power of humans to demonstrate their philanthropy and altruism. In contrast, ontological rejection makes people lose faith and value in just about everything. They reject themselves, others, and the basic value of life. This mindset produces nihilism that usurps normal feelings of humanness.

A more common type of depression is bipolar or manic-depression. It is characterized by mood swings that oscillate back and forth between elation and depression. During mania, when one is elated, feelings of grandiosity, fast speech, impulsive decision-making, and hyperactivity predominate. In a manic state, someone could impulsively spend his entire bank account, talk a mile a minute, feel irritable, and get little sleep. With unipolar depression, where no mania is involved, there is a noticeable absence of life-force energy and one withdraws inward like a turtle retreating into its shell. Conversely, a person in a manic state noticeably expands his life force and begins feeling almost omnipotent. To swing so dramatically between feeling like Superman and not having enough energy to put on one's shoes can be a painful way to live.

Many people with bipolar disorder have shown remarkable displays of creativity and ingenuity due to the surge of energy they experience in the manic state. For example, many historians consider the composer Frederic Chopin to have been bipolar. When I listen to a piece by Chopin, I am filled with a nostalgic, melancholic feeling, a remembrance of the good times from my youth and a yearning to return to some forgotten paradise. I hear the themes of loss, bittersweet sadness, intense romanticism, and a certain kind of introspection. I love classical music and have only discovered this type of music in the last few years. I wonder if Chopin could have written the music he did in a purely unipolar state. It is possible that he wouldn't have had the energy to do so. His manic state might have afforded him the vigor as well as the ability to look into the "telescope of truth" Lord Byron referred to and transform the sadness he felt into fundamental truths about the nature of life that he expressed so beautifully through his piano compositions.

The same might be true for the Russian composer Pyotr Tchaikovsky. By most accounts Tchaikovsky was also bipolar and suffered with the denial of his sexual orientation. The anxieties Tchaikovsky had contributed to several nervous breakdowns as well as a lifelong depression that ultimately consumed him. The music he composed reflects this inner turmoil, especially his Symphony No. 6, "Pathétique." This symphony reflects both the manic and depressive elements that characterized his life, as the composition alternates between a sense of frenzied mania and a mood of heartbreak. In the first movement of this symphony, Tchaikovsky seems to be struggling with his inner demons and the judgments he anticipated if he made known his homosexuality. In the same movement, there is a particularly romantic theme suggesting that Tchaikovsky was yearning for something he could never have, at least in his mind. In the manic third movement, he and the object of his romantic desire triumph before being crushed in the symphony's final movement, which sounds like a sick heart about to stop beating. Interestingly, Tchaikovsky died days after this symphony was first performed. In this symphony, he puts forth the struggles of human existence so forcefully and universally that it seems he, too, had an insider's view of the telescope of truth. It may be true that without the energy of mania to assist him, he could never have composed his symphonies, ballets, and orchestral suites.

For all the creativity and genius that the manic phase can bring, it should not be romanticized. Mania definitely has its dangers, causing people to make poor decisions due to the temporary inflation of the ego. People in this phase are inclined to take extreme financial risks, make poor business decisions, buy expensive items without the necessary funds, and gamble away large sums of money. People in a manic phase should be monitored carefully to ensure their poor judgment does not get them into serious trouble.

There are three types of bipolar depression. Bipolar I is the most serious, involving at least one episode of full-blown mania and at least one episode of major depression or a mixed episode. A mixed episode is when a person experiences both the depressive elements of hopelessness, guilt, and shame simultaneously with the impulsivity, irritability, panic, and suicidal ideation of mania.

Bipolar II isn't as serious as bipolar I. Mood swings do not span the entire spectrum from full-blown mania to major depression. With bipolar II, one experiences hypomania, which is not as intense as mania. A hypomanic state does not produce symptoms of psychosis or the same level of impaired functioning as mania. Yet the same symptoms, such as irritability, higher levels of creativity, impulsivity, and a decreased need for sleep, are present to a lesser degree.

The third disorder on the bipolar spectrum is cyclothymia, a condition even milder than bipolar II. A person diagnosed with cyclothymia may only have peaks that rise to the hypomanic phase and valleys that do not go any lower than dysthymic episodes. But no matter where someone is on the bipolar spectrum, the highs and lows that accompany much of life produce a level of instability that is disconcerting.

Bipolar depression can be co-morbid with Asperger syndrome. Dealing with an unpredictable world coupled with the constant instability of moods is a difficult combination. However, Aspies who are bipolar are in good company. Lynn (2007) makes a persuasive case that the virtuosic pianist Glenn Gould had Asperger's and was also bipolar. In a manic state, Gould used to go running through the Toronto Zoo singing to all the animals. He would also go without sleep for days and had very dark, depressive episodes. Gould was single-minded in his dedication to and interpretation of the music of J. S. Bach, but had a difficult time relating to people. Thomas Edison is another example Lynn offers as an Aspie with bipolar depression. He was someone with very poor people skills and bad hygiene. He had to be reminded to change his clothes. However, in his drive to invent the light bulb, Edison tested over a thousand substances before arriving at tungsten. Many have theorized that the combination of Edison's Aspie-like fixation on electrical design coupled with the intensity of his manic energy may have led to this great scientific breakthrough. Self-awareness is of paramount importance for a person with any type of bipolar depression. The ability to be aware of one's mood shifts is necessary in order to manage this condition.

Pause-and-Reflect Questions

If you have bipolar disorder:

1. What behaviors begin to emerge right before a manic episode?

2. Are you more impulsive and restless?

3. Do you feel a surge of self-confidence that seems to come out of nowhere?

Knowing what triggers a strong mood shift is similar to receiving a tornado warning from the National Weather Service. If you're not aware that a tornado is coming, you may be in its path and get swept up away by it. However, if you have sufficient warning, you can go into the basement and distance yourself from windows and glass, or perhaps drive away from the funnel cloud. The actions you take don't guarantee you won't be affected by the tornado, but the warning certainly reduces the chances of the impact being as severe. The same is true with a manic warning. Mania may suddenly surge unannounced, but watching for signs of the imminent storm will increase the chances that you can mentally and physically slow yourself down to the point where you can catch it in time. Medication, such as a mood stabilizer, can also help. A psychiatrist or your internist can provide guidance on this matter. I will also provide some helpful and user-friendly books on bipolar disorder in Appendix I.

Unfortunately, there is not much written on AS and bipolar depression, but some evidence suggests there could be a connection between the two (DeLong and Dwyer 1988). I hope that more literature will become available and focus on this very important subject.

The suicide rate among those who are bipolar is of great concern. Lynn (2007) cites studies revealing that 15 to 20 percent of adults with bipolar depression had killed themselves and approximately 25 percent of children and adolescents had attempted to do so. As Lynn correctly points out, individuals with Asperger's tend to withdraw when under a great deal of stress so the combination of Asperger's and bipolar depression raises serious concerns. Withdrawing from the life force combined with the energy of mania makes it much more likely that one will attempt or be successful at suicide. People with this combination must be carefully monitored.

Suicidal ideation, which refers to thinking about suicide, is not uncommon with depression. During a serious episode of depression, I once thought about suicide, but when I got to that point, I recognized it wasn't an option and that I needed some kind of assistance. Like most independent Aspies, I don't like asking for help, but when one's life is on the line, it is essential to do so. I have devoted an entire chapter of this book to suicide because of its permanent and devastating consequences. For the *DSM-IV* criteria for major depression and a major depressive episode, see Mental Health Today (no date).

Having Asperger's does not mean you will automatically suffer from depression. A case in point is my cousin, Art, who has Asperger syndrome. He is probably the most content person I know. What allows him to flourish is that he knows how to make his life work for him. The activities that fill his life are an extension of who he is. He loves to cook and has fortunately found a job in the culinary arts as a chef in a restaurant where he is a highly respected and valued employee. He likes to bowl and incorporates that interest in a weekly league. He also enjoys country music and listens to a healthy dose of it each day. He and his father make an annual trip to Nashville to see the Grand Ole Opry. He loves helping people and volunteers many hours each week at his temple serving on committees and helping the homeless. He loves his family and regularly spends time with his grandmother. In short, he isn't wealthy and doesn't have the easiest life in the world, but he genuinely loves his life. I've never heard him complain about anything.

Not all of us can be like my cousin Art, but I mention him because he serves as an example that Asperger's and depression do not necessarily have to go hand in hand. I have met other individuals with Asperger's who also seem very content and happy with their lives. How do they do it? For many of them, I believe their passions and special interests make life worth living. I know this is definitely true for me.

When I feel overwhelmed by the outside world, listening to a Mozart piano sonata takes me to a place where my problems don't exist. Writing also affords me a creative outlet that helps keep me stay balanced and centered. Playing tennis offers me a place to release my aggression and reading helps stimulate my mind. Without my passions and interests, I would be a full-time slave to my worries and problems.

All of us need a certain amount of alone time in order to stay sane in an insane world, but it is important to keep it in balance.

Total disengagement isn't healthy either. My cousin demonstrates a good balance between the absorption in his own interests and a healthy engagement with the external world where true connection can take place. Art would be the first to tell you that he doesn't find it easy to have spontaneous conversations with people, but he doesn't let it bother him. In fact, it's not a real consideration for him. The most important thing for him is to make a connection with people. Even if it is simply saying, "hello," or having a basic exchange, he's content. Another reason Art doesn't get depressed is that he is not introspective. For all of its benefits, too much self-reflection can cause people to view themselves in distorted ways. It's like looking into a microscope. Turning up the magnification a little helps you to see something you might not have noticed without it. But turning up the magnification too high can cause your view to become distorted. You might be hard pressed to recognize the object you were looking at in the first place.

The same is true with analyzing yourself too much. Those with Asperger's tend to be very self-analytical because in a way, they have to be. The world is often such a confusing place that if they can't make sense of it, then at least they can try to make sense of themselves. It's a way of overcompensating for not understanding the world around them. The mind becomes a place of refuge, but when taken to an extreme, this amplification can cause an extremely distorted picture of oneself.

I have described what can happen when the inner critic takes charge. In the next chapter, on cognitive–behavioral therapy, I'll examine how this process takes place and what you can do to change your thinking and change your life.

Chapter 3

Cognitive-Behavioral Therapy

Change your thinking and change your life? That sounds like a tired cliché or the title of some cheesy self-help book on the market today. How could anyone with an M.D. or Ph.D. really understand what a person with Asperger syndrome goes through on a daily basis? How does this expert have the nerve to tell me simply to change my thinking and life will somehow miraculously improve?

While I may not know you or the specific challenges Asperger's creates in your daily life, being an Aspie myself, I get it! I understand how having Asperger's can contribute to a sense of depression. If the first two chapters of this book have resonated with you, I hope you will continue with me while I share a perspective that actually substantiates the statement that if you change your thinking, it actually *can* change your life. The source of my knowledge comes from my own life experience and from my research studies.

The goal of cognitive–behavioral therapy (CBT) is to get people to change the way they think. Sometimes CBT is unjustly criticized because its more orthodox practitioners can seem cold and insensitive in not showing any interest in their clients' past histories. All they want to do is get you to shift your current thoughts to a more positive mindset.

Personally, I like what CBT has to offer, but I also believe that in order to know where you are going, you've also got to understand where you've been. Examining the past, as long as you don't overly magnify or distort it, can be integral in healing parts of yourself and coming to terms with present-day circumstances. I prefer a more moderate form of CBT, in which the therapist is compassionate, and clients are encouraged to take ownership of the past in an effort to change certain thought patterns that may be keeping them stuck in the present.

Milton Erikson, one of the great psychiatrists of the twentieth century, once said that people don't come to therapy to change their pasts, only their futures (Yapko 1997). Barring time travel, it is impossible to go back and change the past. No matter how much you analyze it, it is what it is. In reality, only the present exists as the place to work on a healthier future.

In the heyday of Freudian psychoanalysis, patients would often spend as many as ten years with the same analyst, going as often as three times a week or more, rehashing past events. Ten years is an awful lot of time—not to mention money—to invest in what might or might not produce significant change. While I have benefited from a certain psychoanalytic approach, this type of treatment is primarily a therapy rooted in one's past history. The strength of cognitive–behavioral therapy is that it is entirely a present-oriented therapy designed to help improve not only today, but also the future. When it is combined with an empathetic approach that takes the past into consideration but doesn't overindulge it, CBT can be a powerful catalyst toward positive change and transformation.

A natural part of the human condition is wishing some aspects about one's life were different than they are or were. I certainly wish much of my past was different, and I suspect you do, too. I wish my adolescence had not been so painful, and I wish I would have known how to cope with life better during that time. Although I am an introspective person by nature, I try to strike a balance between examining the past and creating a forward-looking perspective.

In seeking self-improvement and transformation, it is necessary to challenge certain assumptions about yourself that could be holding you back. The basic premise of cognitive–behavioral therapy is that if these maladaptive cognitions or distortions are changed, your behavior will subsequently change. These cognitive distortions slow your life down, make it less efficient, and contribute to depression. Being able to change your thoughts to mirror who you currently are is an effective way to manage depression.

In my book *Asperger Syndrome and Anxiety* (2009), I mentioned the difficulties I had during my student teaching experience. Problems with multitasking and controlling 30 rambunctious second-graders proved to be more than I could handle. When I started my speaking career, I was giving presentations around the country to large groups of parents, educators, and mental health workers. At some point I became aware that despite the success I was having from these speeches, I was always nervous before giving them. It was puzzling. Here I was doing something exceedingly well, but I was still fearful about my ability to give an effective speech.

When I dealt with this issue in therapy, it became clear to me that my thoughts were getting in my way. I began to realize I was carrying the fear from my student teaching experience into my successful speaking career. Instead of focusing on how well my last speech went, I was still thinking about the failure I experienced during my student teaching days. It finally became clear to me that giving a speech to hundreds of interested adults on a subject of great interest to me was very different from teaching 30 second-graders about a subject that was not of interest to me. Once I saw how my past experience didn't really connect to my presentations, I developed a new confidence about this activity. I still feel the anticipatory energy that challenges me to do my best, but now I have confidence in myself to know that all will be well.

I am not saying the struggles you have with Asperger's shouldn't be acknowledged or that these challenges contribute toward your depression. It is important to recognize your limitations and not to deny your emotions. The goal of CBT is to be realistic about which thoughts are currently disproportionate to the present circumstances of your life and to carefully *choose* the thoughts that will help you live the best life possible.

Wait a minute. You might be wondering if you read the earlier sentence correctly. *Choose* which thoughts will help you live the best life possible? The concept that you can actually choose your thoughts may be entirely new to you. I'll admit that it was a revolutionary concept for me about a decade ago. I had no idea that I had the right or capacity to choose my own thoughts and to empower myself in this way.

One way I put this concept to use was in my public-speaking engagements. After I complete a speech, I often get evaluation sheets from the audience. In the past, the minute I got home, I would start to read through these evaluations, looking for any sort of negative remark. I remember after one speech, 79 out of 80 evaluations were extremely positive. Only one was slightly negative. And even the negative one included some positive comments about my presentation. The one negative evaluation focused on the fact that I wasn't able to answer one of the audience's questions. Naturally, I proceeded to obsess about that critical comment for days and made myself perfectly miserable.

What I have since learned is that I can choose the thoughts I want to have. So, instead of choosing to focus on the one evaluation with the critical comment, I would now take note of that comment and, I hope, learn from it, but my focus would be on the positive feedback I received. It's like when you are walking outside on a sunny day with a few clouds in the sky. You can think what a lovely sunny day it is or think too bad it's a cloudy day. There is a rational basis for either thought. It's just a matter of where you want to put the emphasis. Like most things in life, there is usually a basis upon which to draw positive and negative thoughts, but you have control over the area of thought on which to focus your attention.

The truth is that the only person in life who can look out for you is you. Each of us must take responsibility for our own happiness. If we delegate that goal to another person, we will be perpetually unhappy with how that person isn't meeting our needs. If you sabotage yourself with thoughts that deplete your energy, you are being your own worst enemy. It's bad enough that some of us have real enemies in life, so it's best not to be a negative force in your own life. It all comes back to the inner critic. Even though the inner critic lives within each of us at all times, it is not an accurate judge of who we are. Remember, the inner critic's goal is to keep you submissive and insecure with no room to grow.

Have you ever wondered where the inner critic gets these judgments about you? Think about the stereotypical macho football coach who constantly yells at his players but never tells any of them when they are doing well. Or the abusive mother who never takes pride in her children and only focuses on their faults and shortcomings. Believing what the inner critic says is like believing the macho football coach or the abusive mother. The lack of positive encouragement and the negative statements that originally came from people in our past are usually a source of our maladaptive cognitions—thoughts that impede our progress—and now serve as the voice of our inner critic.

My mom told me that when she was a young girl she used to play tennis with her dad. He was an excellent player but not a good teacher, especially with his own daughter. When he would hit the ball to her and she would miss the return, he'd get angry and say things like, "How could you miss that? It was right in front of you!" She said that when she played tennis as an adult and missed a return, she often found herself either thinking or saying out loud, "How could you miss that? It was right in front of you!" Until she was able to see that she had internalized her father's negative comments, she wasn't able to enjoy playing tennis.

Cognitive–behavioral therapy is today's therapy of choice for the management of depression. It has been empirically shown to work with both the AS population and those not on the spectrum. What makes it so effective is that it challenges the inner critic in a logical way and takes apart the faulty assumptions that have governed one's life since early childhood. Using CBT is like finally being able to stand up to an abusive parent whom you've never been able to confront. CBT also helps to get control of the perfectionism inherent in Asperger syndrome.

While I was in middle school, my dad enrolled me on a swim team at our local YMCA. I had taken swimming lessons ever since I was a toddler and had become a decent swimmer. At practice I would swim laps for at least an hour every day. I was on a championship team that had some of the area's best swimmers, but I was in the middle range of my team in terms of talent. At some point during the year, I wanted to quit the team. My dad strongly encouraged me not to quit and to finish the year, which I ultimately did. Before practices, we had many arguments about me staying on the team. When I reflect on why I wanted to quit the team, it wasn't because I hated swimming. What upset me was that I wanted to be one of the best swimmers on the team and I wasn't. My sense of perfectionism would not allow me just to be a decent swimmer. I had to be one of the best. Had I been more psychologically evolved at that time, I would have realized that swimming was a great way to stay in shape, and I didn't have to worry about being the top gun to enjoy being part of a team.

The process of reevaluating past assumptions is not just something that human beings do. Periodically, the collective consciousness has to reappraise belief systems that no longer work for mankind and the world. At one time, it was commonly thought that men were inherently superior to women not only in strength but also in intelligence. Voting laws were structured so that women were not allowed to vote. Women were considered ineligible for certain jobs. When my dad attended law school at the University of Michigan in the 1960s, there were no African-Americans and only about five women in his class of 350 students. In the last 50 years society has begun to rectify the wrongs of racism, sexism, and homophobia. It's hard to believe that less than 150 years ago, slavery existed in the United States, that 50 years ago a black person had to use a separate bathroom in some parts of the South, and that ten years ago, same-sex marriage was unthinkable. If entire nations had blind spots as gaping as these, it makes sense that the same thing would be true for individual human beings.

From where we are now, it is easy to look back at our ancestors and deplore the inhumane ways in which they treated their fellow human beings. Why didn't more people speak out against these injustices? Just think about how future generations might view the inequities that currently exist and are still tolerated.

Hindsight is always 20/20. It's very easy to play Monday morning quarterback *after* unearthing a maladaptive cognition or a faulty belief system that has been governing a nation or ruling one's life since childhood. But until there is a willingness to challenge an existing belief system, that nation or person will be stuck in a state of denial and suffer the consequences.

I know a young man named Pete who has Asperger's. He is inquisitive, kind, and goes out of his way to be friendly to everyone with whom he comes in contact. Every time we happen to cross paths, I genuinely enjoy seeing him. But in some ways, Pete is not an easy person to be around. His view of the world and himself is incredibly pessimistic. He always says that he can never catch a break. He talks endlessly about his family rejecting him and how he can never find a job. He views every situation from a glass-half-empty perspective and feels powerless to be able to improve the circumstances of his life. This is understandable given that he has had many challenges with which to cope in life, but I wish he could see himself the way others see him.

Although he sees himself as a failure, when I look at him I see his many strengths. He is a warm, caring, and enthusiastic man who could accomplish a lot of goals if he had the confidence to do so. For much of his adult life, severe depression has overwhelmed him to the point where he has gone through long stretches of time without seeking employment.

For Pete to raise his level of self-esteem would be an enormous and scary undertaking. It would require him to unearth many years of negative self-talk, bring it all to light, see the illogical nature of it, and then let go of it. To change negative thoughts that one has had since childhood is an extremely difficult challenge. Look how many years it took for the United States to abolish slavery. Even though the abolitionist movement made a strong moral argument against slavery, this institution persisted from the early seventeenth century until the end of the Civil War.

Just as a caterpillar must break free of its cocoon in order to become a butterfly, a person must challenge certain self-limiting beliefs in order to break free of depression. Shedding a part of one's skin or losing a part of one's identity must take place to make room for a new self-image to emerge. Being a caterpillar and staying on the ground is a safer way to go than becoming a butterfly and learning to fly.

It is important to remember there is always pain involved in the birth process. The phrase "birth pangs" describes the pain a woman feels during the transition period of labor from being one with her child to the delivery of a separate human being. Letting go and separating from the criticisms you've heard since childhood and reprogramming your thoughts is not an easy or quick process. You will experience growing pains, but that's a good sign.

In my book *Asperger Syndrome and Anxiety* (2009), I tried to integrate traditional cognitive–behavioral therapy with a more longitudinal approach that takes the past into consideration. Some important books that provide key insights into CBT are David Burns's seminal work *Feeling Good* (1980) and Jeffery Young, Janet Klosko and Marjorie Weishaar's *Schema Therapy* (2003).

Another pioneer of CBT was psychologist Albert Ellis. Ellis was a very shy and timid youngster; as an adolescent, he was petrified of approaching teenage girls and being rejected by them. I've watched sessions of Ellis practicing psychotherapy on the website YouTube and have observed traces of that early social awkwardness. When he was 19 Ellis decided, on a gamble, to speak to over 100 women at a particular gathering. This challenge terrified him, but he wanted to meet this challenge as a way to desensitize himself to his fear of rejection. Ellis overcame this fear of being rejected by women and eventually had a long-term marriage up until the time of his death.

Ellis supported the things he believed in. He did not have an easy life. He suffered from a slew of medical conditions, including diabetes, kidney disease, migraine headaches, and intestinal issues. Just as he coached his clients not to wallow in their misery, he followed his own advice. He was a hard worker well into his late 80s. He was a man who initially struggled with intense social phobias.

Despite these challenges he eventually became, according to the American Psychological Association, the second most influential psychotherapist of the twentieth century.

Some people consider Dr. Ellis's manner in working with his patients to be cold and abrupt. His demeanor did not exude warmth or compassion yet he was enormously effective. No matter how difficult or challenging a person's circumstances were, Dr. Ellis used the same standard formula, called the ABC model. His approach was an offshoot of CBT called rational emotive behavioral therapy (REBT). Ellis's ABC model is quite straightforward:

a. Something happens or a situation occurs.

b. A thought or belief is formed about the situation.

c. There is an emotional reaction to that thought or belief.

Let's take an example to work with that might seem familiar:

a. I have Asperger syndrome.

b. Asperger syndrome limits my chances of obtaining employment, forming a long-term relationship, having a family, and becoming independent from my parents.

c. This thought makes me feel anxious and depressed.

Let's assume Dr. Ellis was working with a young man named Ralph who had Asperger syndrome. Assume further that Ralph expressed the above-stated thoughts. Dr. Ellis would matter-of-factly deconstruct these thoughts employing the ABC equation. He would challenge Ralph's thought that having Asperger's limited his chances at achieving the aforementioned items. For instance, Ellis might ask Ralph if he knew for certain that having Asperger's meant he would never be employed. Ralph would most likely respond that a high percentage of people on the spectrum aren't employed and that he personally hadn't achieved any success so far. Acting dismissive of

Ralph's response, Ellis would then return to his initial question. "But does having Asperger's mean you will *never* be employed? Can you know that for certain?" Ralph might say, "Well, it makes it more likely that I won't be employed," to which Ellis would shoot back, "Okay, so you've acknowledged that not every person in the world with Asperger syndrome is unemployed, correct?" In a calculated move that might appear insensitive, Ellis would actually be trying to instill hope in Ralph. At this moment in the hypothetical exercise, Ralph strongly believes having Asperger's puts all his dreams for employment out of reach. Ellis's approach would be to help Ralph separate fact from fiction. In doing so, Ellis is attempting to get Ralph to rethink his belief system and come to the conclusion that he can possibly be successful in the future and that failure is not inevitable. If Ralph could change his beliefs about the consequences of having Asperger's, his feelings and behavior would inevitably change as a result.

In the example with Ralph, Dr. Ellis was trying to get him to see how his categorical and generalized statements were simply incorrect. By accepting these thoughts as if they were the gospel truth, Ralph was increasing his hopelessness, helplessness, and depression.

Byron Katie and "The Work"

Byron Katie is the writer and best-selling author of a process she developed called "The Work." Her approach is similar to that of Albert Ellis. She suffered from depression and endured some major hardships, which led her to develop a cognitive approach that she claims saved her life. Byron Katie (2003) recounts that for about a decade, she struggled with depression that caused her to hate herself and made her constantly think about suicide. During the last two years of this depression she found it difficult even to leave her bedroom. She was constantly angry with her children and couldn't carry out her basic responsibilities as a parent. She was eventually committed to a mental hospital. In 1986 Katie claims to have had an awakening. This sudden shift produced a realization that it was her thoughts that were keeping her trapped; if she could free herself from these irrational thoughts, she would no longer be depressed.

Katie's process, "The Work" (2003), has much in common with the ABCs of Ellis's rational emotive behavioral therapy. Essentially, her system consists of asking and answering four questions:

1. You have a thought about something. Ask yourself, is that true?

2. Then, can you *absolutely* know that it is true?

3. Then, how do you feel when you believe this thought is true?

4. And finally, who would you be without this thought?

After these four questions have been asked and answered, Katie encourages the person doing "the work" to use what she calls the "turnaround technique," which is to take the person's original thought and turn it into an opposite statement. This turnaround technique is primarily what distinguishes her system from Ellis's approach. Katie takes it one step further by asking the person to reframe the original thought to its complete opposite. And then she will ask for some proof that the inverted statement could be true.

Here's an example of how her process works. For the sake of clarity, I will do "the work" with a thought I will pretend is mine and imagine how Katie would work with that thought.

Me: I can never be successful in the world because I have Asperger syndrome.

Katie: Is this really true?

Me: Yes!

Katie: Can you absolutely know for sure this is true?

Me: Yes. I've read all these statistics in books about how hard it is for people with Asperger's to be employed. Plus I know a lot of people with Asperger's who are out of work and do not function well even when a job is available. So, believe me, I know what I'm talking about.

Katie: How do you feel when you believe the thought, "I can never get ahead in the world because I have Asperger's" to be true? How does your body react?

Me: When I have that thought, I have a sinking feeling in my stomach, my legs feel heavy, and my eyes well up with tears. Actually it makes me want to go eat a couple of pizzas and drown myself in food to avoid the pain this thought always brings. I feel that I will never be an independent person, and I will always have to be at the mercy of others for my very existence.

Katie: Then who would you be without the thought, "I can never get ahead in the world because I have Asperger syndrome"? What if this thought was no longer present in your mind?

Me: I guess for starters, I'd have more energy and more access to my feelings of creativity. I'd have more joy in my life and a lot less fear and anxiety.

Katie: Okay. Now let's try the turnaround technique. How can you turn around the statement, "I can't be a success in the world because I have Asperger's"?

Me: (pausing to reflect) I can be successful in the world because I have Asperger syndrome. Whoa, wait a second? What did I just say?

Katie: Is there any evidence or proof for the statement you just made?

Me: You know, actually, I believe there is. Although not everyone with Asperger's can be a Sir Isaac Newton, Albert Einstein, or an Emily Dickinson, there's a lot of evidence to suggest that creativity, persistence, and a fantastic work ethic exist within the AS population. Integrity, reliability, and the ability to hyperfocus are other desirable traits that, in an ideal world, would trump any of the difficulties those with Asperger's have in the workplace. And sometimes these positive qualities can help in getting ahead in the world.

Katie: So, your statement, "I can be successful in the world because I have Asperger's," has some truth it?

Me: Yes, I guess it really does.

I think Byron Katie's process has some good points, but like most approaches, it is not perfect. Any system that promises to solve all your problems by simply having you answer four questions with a turnaround at the end is a little too good to be true. Most changes in our self-image require more complex analysis than simply asking Katie's four questions. However, I have to admit that when Katie's system works, it works very well. From the previous example, one can see there was a real shift in thinking from helplessness to hopefulness by seriously questioning the thought, "I can't be successful in the world because I have Asperger syndrome." When that thought was turned around to "I can be successful in the world because I have Asperger syndrome," it created a truthful statement that had some proof to support it.

Of course, I am not suggesting that every statement can be turned around so that the opposite of the original negative thought can be shown to be true, but sometimes our minds can be our own worst enemies and by questioning the validity of our thoughts, we can surprise ourselves every now and then. If you examine your thoughts carefully and keep an open mind, you will often discover that the opposite of what you were thinking may be partially if not entirely true.

Here is another example of Katie's turnaround principle from my life:

Me: *Original thought:* I'll never be a good tennis player because I'm short.

Me: *Turnaround thought:* I am a good tennis because I am short.

Katie: Can you provide any proof?

Me: I tend to compensate for my lack of height by having more speed and agility and a keener mind to psyche out my opponents.

Okay, enough about me. How about a turnaround for the late great musician Ray Charles? What if, at age ten, Ray Charles had the thought: I can never be a professional pianist or singer because I'm blind? Of course, someone who had the ability to see into the future could have told him, "Ray, you're going to be one of the greatest musicians in history *because* you are blind. You're going to have access to a dimension of soul and feeling that you might not have had if you could see." Who knows? Perhaps the success of Ray Charles helped Stevie Wonder know that he too could become a major force in the world of popular music.

Some negative self-assessments need to be flipped around and turned inside out. Limitations can be acknowledged without allowing them to define us. Part of being human means having inherent challenges. Some people will have more than others. We are all challenged in some way or to some degree, whether it is socially, economically, or physically.

My personal and professional observations of Aspies are that they usually judge other people based on authentic versus superficial standards. I have also seen that they tend to show more compassion to others than they do toward themselves. If other people make mistakes, Aspies give them the benefit of the doubt, but if *they* make a mistake, they tend to berate themselves. Why are those on the spectrum kinder to others than they are to themselves?

The answer may be that a common trait among those with Asperger's is a sense of excessive self-responsibility (O'Connor 2010). This term refers to the concept that when someone has committed a mistake, he or she judges it much more harshly than if someone else had made the same error. For example, if I was attending someone else's presentation and that speaker couldn't answer one of the audience's questions, I would never think less of that speaker. Yet when I couldn't answer that one audience question at a particular presentation, I beat myself up for it. Intellectually, I know that no one has the answers to every question, but I'm now much more compassionate when it comes to evaluating my own performance.

As you probably know, when you are depressed, there is little or no joy in life. The technical term for this lack of joy is anhedonia, which means the inability to experience pleasure. Anhedonia develops when the feelings of self-loathing associated with negative self-judgments become so intense that a person then indulges in activities such as overeating, compulsive sex, gambling, or drinking as a way to cover up intense feelings of pain. Therefore any potential pleasure associated with these activities gets diluted or eliminated. People who overeat, gamble too often, or use alcohol or drugs too much are not having fun. They are in pain. The beauty of CBT, rational emotive behavioral therapy, and "The Work" is they all force people to come face to face with their self-judgments instead of unconsciously accepting them as the truth.

Cognitive Distortions

This is the part of the chapter where we're going to "get real." Dr. Phil, the popular television talk show host, has a trademark catchphrase he often uses when talking to guests on his program. His advice to "get real" is an effort to give tough love to everyday people like you and me who have difficulty seeing the big picture. Dr. Phil's primary shtick is pointing out faulty, illogical thinking and identifying how cognitive distortions have produced negative life consequences in people's lives.

"How's that working for you?" is another phrase he often uses. When his guests are holding firm to their beliefs and Dr. Phil sees that those beliefs aren't serving any positive function, he'll respond ironically with the question, "How's that working for you?" Although he has a unique style, Dr. Phil isn't really demonstrating any new techniques on his show. The various techniques he employs are used every day in therapy sessions all over the world. Besides his charismatic personality, the public's infatuation with Dr. Phil stems in part from the fact that he practices his form of CBT in an entertaining and forceful manner on a dramatic stage before millions of viewers. Dr. Phil was one of the first psychologists to practice CBT on a national stage. However, there wouldn't be a Dr. Phil without an Albert Ellis, an Aaron Beck, and others who helped to develop and refine this line of psychotherapeutic intervention. Dr. Phil is carrying on the CBT tradition and doing so in an extremely public forum. Although I am not Dr. Phil's biggest fan because I feel he can sometimes be exploitive of his guests, I have to give him credit for making his audience aware of how useful cognitive–behavioral therapy can be in getting people to reexamine their belief systems.

Fortunately, you don't have to be a guest on *Dr. Phil* in order to reprogram your thoughts. This process is a teachable skill. Since around the year 2000, research in the field of brain science has clearly demonstrated that people can learn new ways of thinking later in life thanks to the neuroplasticity—the ability of the brain to rewire its connections (Schwartz 2003). Statements like, "I'm too old to change" or "That's just the way I am" are no longer good excuses for sticking with old thought patterns. Forget about old dogs; you can teach an old person new tricks.

In *Asperger Syndrome and Anxiety* (2009), I discussed the work of the influential psychiatrist David Burns, who is considered to be the successor to Albert Ellis and Aaron Beck. In 1980 cognitive–behavioral therapy had not yet made its way into popular psychology's vernacular. Certainly, it had been written about and practiced by some, but the more Freudian forms of therapy—such as psychoanalysis—were still dominant at that time. Albert Ellis began to garner attention for CBT five years earlier when he wrote the best seller, *A Guide to Rational Living* (Ellis and Harper 1975), which sold more than 1.5 million copies. In 1980, Burns published *Feeling Good*. It has sold close to four million copies to date.

In *Feeling Good*, Burns presented the reader with a series of cognitive distortions or patterns of extreme thinking that appear to be archetypal in nature, meaning we all use them in varying degrees. Since people with depression are predisposed toward negative thinking, Burns observed that these people used these distortions more frequently and to a greater degree than those without depression. Applying this observation to the context of Asperger's, where black-and-white thinking is prevalent, this tendency further increases a person's chances of being unable to see reality accurately. This is not to say that those with Asperger's think less clearly than others, but the inclination to self-degrade is stronger in those who lean toward black-and-white thinking and pessimistic thought patterns.

I am focusing on five of Burns's cognitive distortions (1980) with an emphasis on the interaction between Asperger syndrome and depression. As you read these descriptions, see if any of them seem especially familiar to you.

1. *"Should" statements* make judgments regarding how things should be rather than how they actually are. Psychoanalyst Karen Horney (1950, p.64) called this way of thinking the "tyranny of the shoulds." What she meant was we all have a compulsion to perform according to somewhat perfectionist standards based on our own unique values. For instance, if I am a forceful person by nature, I might think I should always be strong, unemotional, and an overachiever. This particular "should" would be especially difficult to maintain if I ever got sick or had trouble performing a task. Albert Ellis called this style of thinking the "should/must trap" and cleverly coined the term "musturbation" to suggest the obsessive need some people have to ensure things must always go according to plan no matter what the circumstances are.

   Do you have this tendency? Do you get depressed when you are unable to meet your own expectations or when people do not match up with what you expect of them? Conversely, do you get depressed when you are unable to meet the expectations of others? Do you believe it is possible for you to meet the expectations of others all the time? These are not rhetorical questions. Please take some time to reflect on them.

2. *Magnification* is when one only focuses on the negative aspects of an experience while everything else is discounted. Let's say a man named Robert attends a team meeting with his boss and fellow employees. The meeting goes well, and Robert even receives excellent feedback from a co-worker who says she thought what he had to say was helpful and

productive. However, at one point in the meeting Robert had started to make a point but got a little nervous and stuttered. Also, in the middle of the meeting, he had to excuse himself to go to the bathroom. When the meeting is finally over or perhaps even while it is still going on, Robert begins to magnify what he perceives to be the mistakes he made at this meeting (stuttering and leaving to go to the bathroom) and disregards everything else, including the positive feedback he received. Most likely, the behavior that he is concerned about went unnoticed by everyone else.

If magnification is something you do on a regular basis, try to become more aware of it. Remember, you can't change something you're not conscious of. Once you catch yourself doing it, even if it is a couple of days later, try to reframe the situation. Make yourself identify everything you did that went well. Ask yourself if these mistakes were really so bad and if anyone else even noticed them. Ask yourself if someone else made these mistakes, would you think negatively of them? You will, I hope, see that magnification makes you more vulnerable to pessimism and depression.

3. *All-or-nothing thinking* is another name for black-and-white thinking. There is a line from a Billy Joel song called "Shades of Gray" that goes, "Shades of gray wherever I go. The more I find out, the less that I know." Absolutes are comforting but rarely accurate. Socrates said the wise man is the one who admits he is a fool. The more we can admit we don't know the full truth about a situation, the wiser we will be. In most situations, the truth is not always clearly ascertainable. If it were, life would be a lot less mysterious and awesome. Perception wouldn't be as varied, and we would all see things the same way. Everyone would have the same religion, enjoy the same music, dress alike, eat the same foods, and have an equal number of children.

The last two U.S. presidents offered different approaches with respect to all-or-nothing thinking. George W. Bush seemed to be more of a black-and-white thinker. There were certainly fewer shades of gray when he explained a matter of public policy to the nation. Some people liked this style of leadership because it made his views easier to understand. On the other hand, Barack Obama explains the problems facing our country with greater complexity. Some people negatively compare him to Bush in that he appears less decisive. Personally, I prefer his "shades of gray" approach.

All-or-nothing thinking is especially important in terms of self-evaluation. It is critical not to judge others or yourself as being either all good or all bad. Giving others the benefit of the doubt when they act in ways that are less than perfect simply means you are taking the whole person into account rather than evaluating someone based on an isolated incident. Give yourself that same benefit as well. When the self-doubting voice of the inner critic is getting ready to pounce, let the more compassionate side emerge and remind the inner critic that things aren't always so simple.

While going for a walk one evening, a friend of my father's was hit by a drunk driver who left the scene of the accident. It was a shocking and terrible thing to have happened. His friend had to be air-lifted to a trauma center about 40 miles away to deal with the serious injuries he sustained. The young woman who was driving the car was arrested shortly after the accident. She was found passed out on the front lawn of her house. She hardly remembered the accident at all and is currently awaiting trial on serious criminal charges. My dad's friend, who is an English professor and enjoys discussing complex questions, showed the type of thinker he is when he talked about what he thought should happen to this woman. He understands that although young people drink and drive, as he did when he was young, it is still wrong to do so. He isn't angry with her, nor does he intend to demand that she go to jail. Rather, his main concern is that she deals with her drinking problem before she ever gets behind the wheel of a car again. He could easily view this woman as a bad or evil person, considering she almost killed him and left him to die, yet his view is compassionate and filled with shades of gray.

4. *Fortune-telling error* is a negative projection about something that is going to happen in the future even when there is no proof to substantiate the prediction. When someone goes to a stockbroker and asks the broker to analyze his portfolio based on current trends, all the stockbroker can really do is offer an educated guess. While his predictions may turn out to be true, there are other times when his thoughts on the future of the economy may not come to fruition. He is usually making predictions based on how things have gone in the past. But sometimes, as we all know, the market will take a turn for the worse on days you least expect it and vice versa.

   Like the stockbroker, you may forecast how an experience will turn out based solely on past history. Try to become more conscious of when you might be "fortune telling." For instance, the next time you go on a date, even if you have had bad luck with the opposite sex in the past, assume an anything-can-happen attitude and be open to the possibility that romance may bloom or at least you could have a decent time. Depression abates when hope enters the scene. When you predict that bad things are going to happen simply because they may have happened in the past, you are cutting yourself off from any hope of a positive outcome. You don't have to be a Pollyanna and say, "I know this date will be great." Simply hold open space for that possibility.

5. *Emotional reasoning* is thinking only with your emotions. Sometimes emotions can be our best friends. They can provide color and give context to the interior landscapes of our minds as human beings and prevent life from becoming a strictly mechanical exercise. When moving out of a depressive episode, emotions can help to bring us back to life. Without

them, we would be dull, lifeless creatures reduced to nothing more than robots, which is what many people are like when they are depressed. But emotions can also be threatening. Because depressed people feel so little joy, they tend to experience most feelings as painful, whether consciously or not, and need to block their emotional responses. Their goal becomes to repress emotions because they cause pain. Emotions emerge before the neocortex part of the brain even has a chance to process them. Eventually the depressed person thinks, "To hell with this," and gets rid of most, if not all, feelings. Add to this equation the tendency of people with Asperger's to be hypersensitive, and it makes sense that they might want to avoid their feelings entirely.

Even in a psychologically healthy person, there is always the potential for feeling pain. The healthiest way to deal with emotions is to experience them as they come into consciousness. If you are likely to obsess about feelings, this tendency might be one of the reasons you try to insulate yourself from them. You don't want to be engulfed by them.

When you experience an emotion like fear, which causes you to believe the worst possible scenario is imminent, try to get yourself in a more centered place. Remember as a child when you were scared of the monster in the closet, the bogey man under the bed, or some other imaginary character you believed could do you harm? Once you got older and found out these were figments of your imagination, you could laugh at them as well as the emotions they generated.

The same principle that is true for childhood fears also applies to cognitive distortions. Once you understand what's behind the monsters in the closet (your cognitive distortions), it no longer makes sense to be afraid of them. The limbic system—or emotional center—of the brain is so quick to react, it often overrides the higher-order thinking processes of the neocortex, which explains why a dog barks every time he sees or hears the mailman. If the dog had a part of his brain that had evolved like the human brain and allowed him to process the initial emotional response it received, the dog would understand by the third or fourth day that the mailman isn't dangerous. Similarly, the skill of stepping back, taking a deep breath, and calming the sympathetic nervous system must be developed in order to slow down, gain clarity, and logically decide a next step. This course of action prevents reactive behavior.

There was a story in the newspaper about a man who was driving his car and had stopped for a red light when a carjacker forced him out of his car and drove away. The man was so angry he started chasing after the car and shot at it with a gun he was licensed to carry. Unfortunately the bullet went astray and entered the house of an elderly woman who was in the process of cooking dinner. The bullet entered this woman's head and she immediately died. The victim of the carjacking was then charged with involuntary manslaughter in that he acted in a grossly negligent manner in the discharge of a firearm. Had the man calmed himself down for even a few seconds, he would have realized that he was no longer in any physical danger and that he should call the police. Ideally, they could have apprehended the criminal and returned his car to him. If the car had been damaged, he even had insurance to cover his loss. Because of his quick and intense emotional response, he is now facing serious felony charges. The carjacker was also charged with felony murder of the elderly woman. Granted, this is an extreme example of reactivity with life and death consequences, but when we think only with our emotions, we tend to create serious problems for ourselves.

Breaking out of these habitual cognitive distortions into a more evolved kind of thinking can be liberating. It is like removing a pair of dirty, scratched glasses and putting on new glasses with clean lenses that allow you to see everything with clarity. You might even get to the point where you say to yourself, "I can't believe I let my thoughts rule me for so long." But instead of using that thought against yourself (as the inner critic would surely love), you can just chalk it up to being part of your self-improvement process for growth, development, and transformation.

Schemas

Consider the fact that during the first six years of life, a child's brain is in the Delta, Theta or Alpha brain states, which interestingly corresponds to a hypnotic trance one would be put in by a stage hypnotist! This is partially why the behaviorist John Watson felt he could shape an infant to become anyone he wanted if given the opportunity. The Jesuits were similarly aware of this impressionable state when they decreed that they could take any child up until the age of seven and determine the kind of person they would become (Lipton and Bhaerman 2009).

If the human mind is like a hard drive on a computer, human experience is the software. When unpleasant experiences repeat themselves, they set up "programs" that tell the operating system (hard drive) how to run. This is also true with pleasant experiences. When we receive positive reinforcement and have success, it builds positive programs that enhance self-esteem. But sometimes a foreign agent (virus) can attack the operating system and the result is that it shuts down.

If our minds are like hard drives, then these viruses can come in many shapes and sizes, but they are all toxic outside agents that can do harm. A virus can arrive in the form of a perceived or real criticism, a death in the family, the loss of a job, or the failure to pass an exam. Whatever the situation may be, viruses create programs that can wreak havoc on the hard drive and cause it to slow down or come to a complete halt. Fortunately, there are "system mechanics" and "antivirus software" like we use with computers that protect the mind from environmental influences and keep it running smoothly.

A self-schema is a thought pattern about oneself that was probably acquired in childhood and has been reinforced in adulthood. When these thought patterns operate without awareness, they can cause great damage, like a virus in a computer. A self-schema operates like the fictional wizard of Oz who is controlling the levers and hiding behind the curtain. When these self-schemas are examined and seen for what they really are, it is like Toto the dog pulling back the curtain and exposing something harmless that was previously frightening.

What if one of your self-schemas is, "I cannot function competently in the world"? Assume this belief has been your modus operandi for years, but you haven't been consciously aware of its existence or that it is causing you any harm. If that is the case, you would approach situations with this core belief of your inability to cope with most situations, influencing almost everything you do and making the world appear very threatening. Without an examination of this self-schema and its utility, there is no ability to delete it from your mind (hard drive).

In *Asperger Syndrome and Anxiety* (2009), I identified a number of schemas that were common in the AS population, based on both anecdotal experience and research. These core beliefs create suffering and contribute to depression. Here are those schemas:

- People cannot be trusted.

- I cannot function adequately in the world.

- Things are either good or bad.

- I am inherently worthless. I have worth only when others approve of me.

- The world is unpredictable and unsafe.

It is important to scrutinize each of these beliefs carefully and decide whether you honestly believe them to be true, and if so, to what degree. If you do subscribe to any one of the above schemas, you should have a plan of action that will confront these distortions.

I won't try to argue with your sense of reality. If you believe you cannot function adequately in the world, I would certainly empathize with that feeling, being a person with Asperger's myself. But after showing some compassion for your view, I would ask whether or not you want to continue to maintain this belief. One might presume the answer to that question would be "no," but for many people, there is comfort in holding on to a self-schema because it justifies not taking any risks or experiencing the possibility of failure.

My dad is a successful lawyer. For a number of years, he was a trial lawyer and is now a law professor. He is often on television as an analyst for legal events that occur locally and nationally. He told me that when he was in high school, he never participated in any extracurricular activities. He really wanted to be on the debate team, but he didn't even try out. *He didn't think he was good enough to make the grade.* Now that he has attained significant professional achievement, he realizes his view of himself (the self-schema) was unrealistic and he would have probably been successful in many high school activities. He told me how sad he is about not having tested himself in high school. My dad eventually reevaluated that self-schema after high school and took on many challenges throughout college, law school, and in his professional pursuits as a lawyer.

Fortunately, there's usually another part of our psyches that is dormant but still wants to challenge the core belief of inadequacy. Try to get in touch with that part of yourself that knows you are a decent, competent, and energetic person who can make a positive difference in the world by virtue of your individuality. I believe that's what happened to my dad and also what happened to me when I began my doctoral degree.

After I was accepted into a doctoral program in psychology, I became extremely fearful and overwhelmed. I worried about how I could ever complete five years of intensive study, fulfill two internships, and write a doctoral dissertation to graduate with my doctoral degree. My self-schemas took over without my even being aware of it, and I became paralyzed with self-doubt. I had convinced myself that my acceptance into the program was a mistake or some kind of a fluke, and I was going to fail. Luckily, another part of me eventually emerged that was willing to challenge the self-schema that my acceptance was a fluke. I was finally able to see that it was because I had earned the appropriate credentials for admission and the school believed I could reach my goal. Now that I have successfully graduated from the program and earned my doctorate in psychology, I can acknowledge that my fear about being successful was not rational or warranted. The school accepted me for the right reasons. Had I not been able to challenge my self-schema, I might have dropped out of the program.

I believe most people have the desire to bring the best parts of themselves out of hibernation and into their active lives. In the 1960s President John F. Kennedy challenged the United States to go to the moon by the end of the decade. Such a journey had never been tried, but the country got behind the president's positive vision and ended up accomplishing this seemingly impossible goal. Kennedy knew most people would want to support this challenge because it reflected the best part of our human nature.

Here is a worthwhile exercise: make a list of some of your self-schemas, whether positive or negative. Then examine each one through a process of inquiry involving four questions. This method is a blend of Ellis's REBT and Byron Katie's "The Work." Here is an example:

I am a bad soccer player.

Now ask yourself four questions:

1. Is this belief true?

   (I can honestly say that for me, it is true.)

2. Does the belief have utility? In other words, does focusing on this belief have significance in defining my sense of self?

   (In my case, no. This thought does not enhance my sense of existence, nor does it fill me with dread. Even though the belief is an accurate statement of fact, it serves no purpose in making life better for me.)

3. Does this belief reinforce my depression?

   (If I generalize from it and feel that I have no athletics skills, it most certainly would.)

4. Even if this belief is true, is it especially relevant to my life?

   (No, it isn't.)

This example was overly simplistic. Let's use one that is more relevant to people with Asperger's:

I am not good at socializing.

1. Is this belief true?

   (I would say that socializing isn't one of my strong points.)

2. Does the belief have utility?

   (The only usefulness of this belief is it allows me to take inventory of my strengths and challenges as a human being. Other than that, dwelling on my belief that social situations can be challenging could lower my self-esteem.)

3. Does this belief reinforce my depression?

   (If I allowed myself to be defined by this belief, it certainly could.)

4. Even if this belief is true, does it have to be especially relevant to my life?

(Not really. On the surface it would seem that the ability to socialize gracefully and effectively is extremely relevant to a happy life. Jobs, livelihood, friendships, and romantic relationships all depend on this skill. Yet some of the most socially awkward people have ended up being extremely successful in life. Those people found a way not to let themselves be defined or defeated by their social ineptness. Depending on their insight and resourcefulness, they might have even found unconventional ways of using their social awkwardness to their advantage.)

When practicing cognitive–behavioral therapy, it's important to become aware of how making generalized statements about one's personal deficiencies can reduce self-esteem. A thought like "I'm not good at socializing" can lead to an even more generalized belief like "I cannot function adequately in the world." While a person may not feel comfortable in social situations and can admit there's some truth to that fact, the notion of generalized inadequacy—which your inner critic wants you to believe—still needs to be challenged.

The goal of an action plan should be to minimize the relevance of a particular schema through both thought and action. If a particular belief has been examined and found to have no usefulness, then it's time to minimize its relevance.

During my internship in graduate school, I met with a man named Paul who was in his late 20s and had Asperger's. He would constantly talk about his rocky relationship with his father. It sounded like he had done everything in his power to have a relationship with his dad, but there was no reciprocal interest. Additionally, Paul felt a strain with other family members who were not providing him with the love and nurturance he sought. I sensed that Paul was somehow contributing to the tension between himself and his father. However, after pressing the issue for some time and getting more information, I reached a different conclusion. I saw that Paul's dad was mostly to blame. Paul had actually been a very good son and had tried repeatedly to connect with his dad. He asked very little of his father other than wanting his love and respect.

I attempted to show Paul empathy for his painful feelings about his relationship with his father. Week after week we discussed Paul's concerns. I felt his pain. At first I made the assumption that empathy was what Paul needed from me because I thought I was the only person in his life who understood what he was going through. I assumed that if I were the one sitting in Paul's chair, I would want to have my feelings about my father validated. What I came to discover was empathy only helped to a point. Even after showing Paul that I understood how he felt, I noticed his level of distress about the situation did not diminish. If anything, after a while my empathy seemed to fuel his depression. The more I empathized with him, the more upset he became in solidifying his belief that this important but unsatisfying relationship with his dad was never going to change. I couldn't believe it, but my continued empathy was actually increasing his despair. As an intern in training (who clearly had a lot to learn), I saw that I needed to take a different approach if I wanted to be helpful to Paul.

I was beginning to see that unless I developed some sort of action plan Paul could follow, nothing else was going to help him. I now realized that my task was to help Paul cognitively restructure the level of importance he attached to his relationship with his father. I needed him to understand that part of what was causing his distress was how much he had invested in the importance of this relationship when he wasn't getting anything back in return. I asked Paul to imagine what his life would be like if he attached less importance (or relevance) to his father's lack of connection with him. At first, he was livid that I would even make such a callous remark. How could I be so insensitive? Eventually Paul began to see that part of what was making him so miserable was the degree of significance he attached to his father's lack of concern for him.

No one can dispute how painful it is to have a cold and distant parent. But after a while the question for Paul changed: how much was he going to let this unfortunate situation rule his life? I encouraged Paul to find meaningful relationships with other people and get his emotional needs met from them rather than his father. Although this was not easy, he has since done so and is a lot less miserable than he was.

Like Paul, who attached too much importance to having a relationship with his dad, people with Asperger's frequently place too much significance on their lack of social skills. In order to minimize the relevance of that schema in your life, you would need an action plan. You might start by contemplating what you could do to make socializing less important in your life. Perhaps you could work at a company that is known for having a tolerant and flexible working environment, where you could disclose your social limitations and others might be more understanding of your needs. On a smaller scale, you could decide to leave social gatherings a little early and choose not to feel guilty about it. You might also look for a group to join that is based on your special interests. These are only suggestions. The important point is to find ways to help you meet your social needs without having to experience a lot of frustration. Instead of focusing on people or situations in your life who are not meeting your needs, or in which you have little or no control, try to develop a plan in which you can find alternative ways to meet these needs.

It is helpful to be aware of our limitations, but facing these unpleasant truths doesn't mean wallowing in them or letting them define us. On the contrary, being honest with oneself can help diminish the importance of these perceived weaknesses and be the first step toward self-acceptance.

In second grade I was diagnosed with a learning disability in written expression. My fine motor skills were so poor that my handwriting was almost impossible to read and art class was tortuous for me. At the time, computers were not widely used so this disability seemed fairly dire in terms of my future educational success. During the next few years as computers became more available in the schools and I got my own computer, writing was no longer a problem for me, and this learning disability was expunged from my record. It is ironic that someone who received an early diagnosis of a learning disability in written expression now has to his credit three published books that are distributed throughout the world.

Self-acceptance can be difficult for Aspies who tend to fixate on their perceived weaknesses, but the ability to seek change requires an act of courage. It is important to acknowledge uncomfortable self-schemas while at the same time withholding judgments about them.

Pause-and-Reflect Questions

1. Is the self-schema or belief I'm thinking about true?

2. Even if it is true, does the schema have utility—that is, does it work for me?

3. Is this schema reinforcing my depression?

4. Even if this schema is true, is it relevant to my life?

5. What kind of action plan can I take to diminish the importance of this belief or schema?

The most significant point to remember is many of these self-schemas are thoughts that have been around since childhood and are simply no longer true. You've outgrown them, but you might not be aware of that fact unless you question the belief. Because these schemas have been part of a pattern of thinking for such a long time, they are not going to go away without a fight. Therefore, these thoughts must be seriously challenged to determine their current relevance or utility.

Implementing the material in this chapter will be challenging. Having a therapist to work on these issues with you would be ideal. Take it one step at a time to avoid being overwhelmed. Celebrate small insights as they lead to larger ones. And above all, be compassionate with yourself as you go through this process.

Chapter 4

The Dark Night of the Soul

I want to introduce a concept that has some spiritual overtones. I hope no one is offended by the word "spiritual." I respect everyone's belief system including those who don't believe in a higher power and have no personal investment in anyone's belief about the nature of the universe.

Have you ever wondered why some prisoners have conversion experiences while serving their terms of incarceration and suddenly become religious? Prison would seem the least likely environment for such an event to occur. Or have you ever speculated on why some people who aren't religious throughout their lives have intense spiritual experiences when they are going through the process of dying? And have you thought about why alcoholics often have to hit rock bottom before they are open to an intervention? Why do these people all need to be at their breaking points or even close to death before they can finally attempt to undergo a major change?

To help answer those questions, I want to share one of my own dark nights of the soul that I experienced in 2003. I was on the verge of completing a master's degree in special education. Having been an average student in high school, I never thought I could have accomplished such a goal. My future was looking bright, and I was about to graduate with a magna cum laude distinction on my graduate transcript. At the time, it seemed like nothing could prevent me from fulfilling my career objective of becoming a special education teacher. I was looking forward to this new path and also righting the wrongs of some of the teachers I had in elementary school. I was at the peak of having attained academic success.

The only obstacle before me was passing the student teaching requirement since all of my class work had been successfully completed. I distinctly remember my first day of student teaching. I pulled into the parking lot of the school and suddenly felt incredibly nauseous. It was almost as if I knew at a deep level that something didn't feel right, but I couldn't put my finger on what it was. Maybe I was just having cold feet. All I knew was that whatever I had signed up for, I now wanted out! Considering I had come this far, I figured I had no choice but to complete the last leg of the journey or I would risk negating everything I had achieved in the last three years.

As I walked into the school I began to sweat profusely. In retrospect I believe I was having a mini panic attack. I was actually starting to hyperventilate when I saw hundreds of children running down the halls and making a lot of commotion. I saw a group of teachers schmoozing while sitting around the teacher's lounge. Everything about this setting appeared so foreign to me. What was I doing here? I kept thinking this is not where I could see myself spending the next 30 years of my life.

From the very first day, bad things immediately started to happen. I couldn't do anything right. My cooperating teacher was constantly criticizing me, even when I was trying my best, like when I couldn't tie a piece of string and hang it from the ceiling for a science project, or when I accidentally broke the school's laminating machine. I felt I needed eyes in the back of my head since I lacked the perceptual abilities to keep track of all the activities with which 30 second-graders were involved in this busy classroom. It was my responsibility to remember all of them. It got so bad that on some days I even forgot to pick up the children from their special classes, like gym, art, and music.

Everything seemed to be working against me, with each passing day being worse than the one before. One day I was so overwhelmed that a school staff person actually caught me in an empty room lying on the floor in an exhausted state. This experience was draining me of all my energy, and I was starting to give up without realizing it. Six weeks after I began student teaching, the principal and my cooperating teacher said they needed to talk to me regarding my future as a student teacher. They arranged a meeting that included the two of them, a special education teacher with whom I was planning on working the following semester, my university supervisor, and me. Before I even walked into the principal's office, I knew in my heart what the outcome of this meeting was going to be, and I knew it was probably the best for everyone concerned. As I had sensed, they all had come to the clear conclusion that my teaching elementary school wasn't a good fit and that I should start looking into other career options. I felt like an instant failure. Three years of schooling and a whole lot of money down the drain, with nothing to show for it other than a master's degree that wouldn't even get me a job at a tutoring center because I lacked a teaching certificate. During this same time period, I was also diagnosed with type 2 diabetes. I felt as if the world was sending me some very negative messages.

I was in an existential crisis of monumental proportions. Suddenly, my life had no direction and was without meaning. I was facing what I perceived to be an uncaring world in which I was completely ill-equipped for the job market in spite of all my years of education. I felt destined to be overeducated and unemployable. I stayed in my apartment in a kind of self-imposed exile, with the exception of getting food and occasionally seeing my parents. During this four- to five-month period, I slept very little, ate too much, and from time to time had fleeting thoughts of suicide.

At some point I had to come face to face with my inner and outer demons. My endocrinologist informed me that if I did not begin taking better care of myself, I was going to become extremely ill. This grim news ironically offered a strange sense of relief in that my suffering might come to an end sooner rather than later. However, being told that I had a chronic medical condition that could create all sorts of nasty complications like blindness, loss of limbs, and kidney failure definitely put the fear of God into me. Although dying seemed to have its benefits, long-term suffering and being incapacitated by grave illness sounded like a living hell. I didn't really have to consider suicide because it looked like my body was going to take care of that on its own. With all the weight I was gaining and the health problems I was accumulating, my body, mind, and spirit were all on a sharp decline.

I was forced to make a choice. Did I want to live or die? Intellectually, the answer was relatively easy. At that time I wanted to die, but there was something that kept me from implementing that option. Perhaps unconsciously, I sensed it was necessary for me to go through an intense period of suffering so I could come out the other side with some wisdom to show for it.

My depression peaked, and I even began to realize that my death would mean that I would never again see my parents. I believed that loss might have been a necessary price to pay to escape the bleak existence that was in store for me over the next 50 or 60 years. Part of the reason why I felt such despair was knowing my parents would die some day, leaving me alone without any other family to rely on. Since I am an only child, the thought of possibly being alone at the end of my life was unbearable. It seemed that there was no way my life could have a happy ending.

What began as a failed student teaching experience had spiraled down into a deep, dark journey from which it seemed I could not escape. It was like I had fallen down a giant hole and there was no way of getting out. I began to ask myself some fundamental questions about life: Why am I here? What is the point of my existence? How will my life end? Is there a God? Why doesn't God offer me some help or protection? Is life worth living? Will my suffering ever end?

There was no response to these questions. I felt totally abandoned by any kind of higher power that might exist. I was angry that God could put so many obstacles in my way and expect me to handle all of them. I was even angry that God made me so weird. A barrage of thoughts flooded my mind. Why had I never been able to make and keep friends? Why didn't I have much in common with my peers? What kind of God would create a person who was so different and subject him to such a cruel and uncaring world? I began to wonder if God even had a perverse side and actually enjoyed watching certain human beings suffer. I also considered that perhaps I had done something horrible in a past life and this was my retributive karma coming back at me. I wasn't ruling anything out.

The "big black dog" of depression—as Winston Churchill famously described his own illness—was nipping at my heels and I couldn't find any way to shake him loose. Music wasn't offering me the solace it usually did. My "stims" or repetitive activities—like watching the same tennis match over and over—didn't restore my sense of equilibrium. The things I had counted on for years to get me through bad moments were no longer providing me refuge. I was having the experience that St. John of the Cross described in his writings as "the dark night of the soul."

In 1577, St. John was captured and held in solitary confinement for nine months in Spain. Most of his life had been devoted to service and spiritual contemplation. When he was taken prisoner, he was stripped of everything meaningful and placed in a tiny cell. The only human contact he had was with a guard who would beat him on occasion. Suddenly derailed from the work that meant so much to him, he fell into a deep depression.

Like St. John, I felt suddenly derailed from my career path and began to live my life as if it were in a tiny cell. I plunged into the depths of despair, which included extreme sensory deprivation. I closed all the windows in my condo and kept the lights off, denying myself anything pleasurable. I had no contact with anyone outside of my parents. This was indeed my dark night of the soul.

Earlier I referred to Viktor Frankl, who was imprisoned in the Auschwitz death camp during the Second World War. He was separated from his wife and forced to watch his fellow prisoners die in the most unimaginable, inhumane ways possible while waiting for his own death to occur. Despite the impossible conditions under which he lived, something within him wanted to survive. That same inner strength could also explain the remarkable survival of Nelson Mandela, Ludwig van Beethoven, Swiss psychiatrist Carl Jung, and even singer songwriter Billy Joel, all of whom suffered from severe depression only to emerge with renewed strength and purpose.

Billy Joel was down on his luck as a young singer and composer when he and a fellow musician put out an album that was a disastrous flop (Bordowitz 2006). Joel knew that his purpose in life was to make people happy by composing and playing music, but his talents went unnoticed. Since no one was recognizing him for the musical genius that he was, he went into a major depressive state. Following a failed suicide attempt he checked himself into a mental hospital. Once there he entered a world that frightened him even more. With the cacophony of human voices coming from all directions, Joel started to doubt whether he belonged in a mental institution. Although he received psychiatric counseling for his depression while he was there, he ultimately came to the conclusion that his life really wasn't as bad as he thought. It took a stay in a mental hospital for him to come to this realization. Would he have had this awareness without being hospitalized? No one can say. Like most of us, it seems he had to hit rock bottom before he could be open to a new perspective about his life. Joel shares the lessons he learned about depression in a famous song he wrote aimed at young people who are disillusioned and depressed, called "You're Only Human (Second Wind)." Joel has had his share of personal troubles since making it big in the music industry, but it was only after his dark night of the soul that he finally solidified his purpose in life. When he surrendered to what was and not what he wanted life to be, he was finally able to succeed in elevating his mood. When he became grateful for his health and his musical talents, he could appreciate his life as it was and proceed to maximize his skills in becoming the superstar that he is today. His contentment with life helped him sweep away his depression and let him achieve bigger and better results as a professional musician.

Another musical genius who was transformed as a result of a deep depression was Ludwig van Beethoven. Imagine what it would have been like to lose your hearing when your greatest passion in life was composing music. Beethoven's hearing loss was a devastating blow. When his hearing began to decline, he went from doctor to doctor in a frantic search to find a cure. Despite every doctor's best effort to help, his hearing was almost completely gone by the time he was 32. Given his hopeless diagnosis, Beethoven totally isolated himself, leading to his dark night of the soul. During this time, the composer was very depressed and seriously considered suicide, but the sound of the music was still stirring inside him. The sounds he was hearing from memory were too great to ignore, even if he couldn't actually hear the music he composed when it was being played. Beethoven once said, "It seemed impossible for me to leave the world until I had brought forth all that was in me" (Armstrong 2010, p.103). Following the period of his dark night, he went on to compose the groundbreaking Symphony No. 3. This single symphony essentially ushered in the transition from the classical era into the romantic era of classical music. The romantic era music is characterized by depth of emotion, passion, and very expressive tones, unlike the classical era that was more about tuneful balance, and control. These romantic qualities seemed to become increasingly evident in Beethoven's music as his hearing declined. Once Beethoven made peace with his hearing loss and stopped feeling depressed, he became one of the most pivotal composers in classical music history. Without his dark night, would this have been possible?

My dark night of the soul ended much the same way as Beethoven's. When I could finally accept and even embrace the very things that had sent me into depression, I began to emerge from it. I am convinced that if it hadn't been for the disastrous student teaching assignment, my life would have taken a very different trajectory. In fact, I would go so far as to say that I *needed* that dark-night experience in order to move forward. I needed to be shaken to my core in order to revise a very outdated belief system that was fueling my depression.

After the student teaching disaster, I started to wonder if something else was involved that might explain why I had failed so miserably. There had been other unexplained events in my life so this was not the first. I wanted to find out if there were any other diagnoses that could have been missed by the series of professionals I had worked with in the past. At the time, I was taking a course in abnormal psychology and threw myself into learning as much as possible about this subject. After only about a month in this class, I read about Asperger syndrome.

Despite the fact that I had worked with several different psychologists and psychiatrists over the years, no one had ever mentioned this particular diagnosis. Different labels had been suggested from time to time, but they had been subsequently eliminated. The more I read about Asperger's, the more convinced I was that this was the missing piece that could explain my personal life puzzle.

After I had read several books and articles on Asperger's, I shared this information with my parents, thinking they would be overjoyed with my discovery. They were not. They read all the information I gave them but still didn't think that it applied to me. My mother thought that it was common to take a psychology class and identify with all the different diagnoses. For the next month or so, I continued to send them more articles and they continued to deny the overwhelming evidence that I was presenting to them. I knew this diagnosis was correct, and I needed to convince them. Finally my parents and I went to the psychiatrist I had been seeing for several years. He said he had never even considered that I had Asperger's, and then he asked what difference it would make if I did. He said I would just have a name for a cluster of characteristics that I had. I was very unhappy with his response. I felt he was being dismissive of a potentially major discovery in my life. I then went to the psychologist whom I had been seeing for therapy. He also said he had never considered Asperger's as a diagnosis for me but encouraged me to get evaluated by a neuropsychologist, which I then did.

After three sessions of testing that took a total of ten hours, the neuropsychologist confirmed that I indeed had a classic case of Asperger syndrome. I was tremendously relieved to hear this conclusion and by that time so were my parents. Subsequently, I went to another psychologist for a second opinion so there would be no doubt about the accuracy of the diagnosis, which she confirmed. As glad as I was to have a name for my condition as well as an explanation for so much confusion in my life, I now had to face the fact that I was on the autism spectrum.

My dark night of the soul had taken me to the darkest places I had ever been but ultimately brought me much-needed clarity. The question now confronting me was: would I be able to shed this mountain of negativity from my past and be open to new ways of seeing myself? I felt like I was trying to hold on to a blanket from childhood that had brought me safety and security and I didn't want to let go of it. The dark-night experience demanded that I forfeit the blanket without promising anything in return. Psychiatrist and Holotropic Breathwork™ pioneer Stanislav Grof and his wife Christina Grof (1992) point out that when a dark night takes place, it flips your world upside down and forces you to change your perceptions.

As a result of my dark night, I had a few stunning realizations that left me breathless. The most important was that I actually had Asperger syndrome. The qualities in myself that I had detested all my life were now the very qualities my soul was asking me to embrace. I understood that there was a part of me that actually had to die for another part to be born. I had to let go of the part of myself that believed I had to conform to the expectations of others and, instead, accept who I really was and live congruently with this new self. I had to come to terms with the fact that I was never going to have a typical job. I knew I would have to find my own unique path in life.

During my dark night, I struggled against the concept of self-acceptance. Why would I want to reveal myself in all my glory when those were the very qualities that had always gotten me in trouble in the past? It just seemed so damned counterintuitive. But alone in that dark tunnel without any sign of light at the end, I was willing to try anything since nothing else had worked.

A few years passed and the process of change was beginning to take hold. I was coming to terms with my diagnosis, starting a doctoral program in psychology, beginning to speak at conferences throughout the United States, writing journal articles and books, and a whole lot of other things I never would have dreamed possible. But none of it would have happened unless I did what I was asked to do in the dark night of the soul: accept myself for who I was.

The dark night of the soul can be seen in action everywhere. A movie star's dark night could be the realization that someday she will no longer have a young, hot-looking body, no matter how much she exercises or diets, or the amount of plastic surgery she undergoes. Her resolution may be to accept that she is more than just her body. A Wall Street investor's dark night could have easily taken place in 2008 when the stock market took a colossal nosedive. Perhaps the lesson he might have to learn is that a meaningful life is still possible without having a lot of money.

A dark night could occur when a drug addict may lose his wife and children as a result of his addiction unless he decides to change his life. It can happen when people get a life-threatening illness like cancer or heart disease and after going through all the stages of denial, bargaining, anger, and so on are able to make peace with the diagnosis and live the reminder of their lives with more joy and zest than they previously had.

The dark night is often dramatized in films. In *The Wizard of Oz* the tornado that hits Kansas symbolizes the beginning of the dark night; the journey through the Land of Oz represents Dorothy's transformation as the light of day comes into view at the end when she returns Kansas and realizes, "There's no place like home."

The Truman Show, starring Jim Carrey, is another example of a character that goes through a dark night in order to achieve change. Carrey plays Truman Burbank, an unsuspecting reality television star whose entire life has been videotaped and broadcast to a world audience, but he is not aware of that fact. Everyone who interacts with him is really a paid actor in a gigantic television studio built exclusively for the show, but Truman believes it is his real life. As the movie goes on, Truman slowly starts suspecting that his perceptions of his life are not quite right but he can't put his finger on why. The tension escalates between Truman and the other characters who continually try to conceal their true identities from him, while the show's creators make it virtually impossible for Truman to believe that he can ever leave Sea Haven Island, the fictitious place where he lives. Truman's anger and depression build throughout the film as he realizes he must leave the island but is unable to do so, no matter how hard he tries. Finally out of desperation, he somehow sneaks out when the cameras aren't looking and faces his lifelong fear—the ocean. This fear developed when Truman was a child and the show's creator and producers organized a "death at sea" episode where Truman and his father went boating together and his father drowned. This scene was created intentionally so Truman would never try to escape from his island studio.

The creator of the show, who is supposed to represent God, discovers that Truman is out on the ocean in front of a worldwide audience, and attempts to drown him by creating a vicious tropical storm. Truman wants to turn back because of his lifelong fear of the water, but he decides that this time he is going to plunge ahead (pardon the pun). When Truman's boat tips over, he heroically climbs back in and sails to the end of the soundstage where he is met by the show's creator who tells him he doesn't have the guts to leave the show and tries to convince him that the real world is actually worse than the one in which he currently lives. With a bow and a smirk, Truman decides otherwise and gracefully exits the studio to live his real life, unencumbered by the burden of entertaining a worldwide audience any longer.

Truman's depression stemmed from the fact that he knew he wasn't living an authentic life and felt powerless to do anything about it. The more he tried to be content living in this false world, the more his inner voice tugged at him, telling him he was missing out on something real. Truman felt his miserable life on Sea Haven Island was going to last forever, and it might have, had he not gone through with his dark night in which he learned to appreciate all the virtues that real life has to offer. Without the experience on Sea Haven Island, perhaps Truman would have taken life for granted just as many of us tend to do.

The reference to the dark night also seems to reflect a principle of nature. The darkness of winter gives way to the renewal of spring. The darkest hour occurs right before the dawn. Many people who have had near-death experiences talk about the transformative effects those experiences had on their lives. Life is all about cycles, and sometimes journeys to the depths are necessary so that one can rise up with more wisdom than one previously had. No dark night is ever permanent. Whether by design or circumstances, the one constant throughout time is that life will always change.

A dark night is a lot like an army drill instructor who might shake a young cadet to his core while at the same time teach him how to be better prepared to go out and do battle. Being forcefully told to change your ways or risk not being able to survive might be difficult for the cadet to hear, but eventually he will be rewarded. When defending himself and his country, he will be more equipped to handle the life and death situations he will have to face in the future. The armed forces are rare environments in which sometimes being humiliated and taken apart can paradoxically help to build one back up even stronger than before. This type of growth process was certainly illustrated in the films *An Officer and a Gentleman* with Richard Gere and *Private Benjamin* with Goldie Hawn.

If the dark-night experience demands one thing, it is change. For people with Asperger's, change is especially difficult. An important point to remember is that as long as a person is resistant to change, the dark night may last longer than necessary.

The Dark Night of the Soul and Asperger's

There are many factors that lead into a dark night, but those with Asperger's are especially vulnerable to its depths of despair. That's the bad news. The good news is that Aspies are in a position to gain more personal growth if they are open to accepting the possible rewards the dark night has to offer.

Why are those with Asperger's more susceptible to dark nights? One explanation is they are more prone to problems with employment, relationships, and transitioning into adulthood. These are issues that neurotypicals also face, but can deal with more easily (Stoddart 2005). Being depressed in response to the loss of a job or the end of a relationship can force us to question the ontological purpose of our lives. When we have racked up enough failures, we will inevitably raise questions about our lack of self-worth, along with pleas to God in the middle of the night.

During a dark-night period, it's important for those with Asperger's to be particularly conscious of their tendency to obsess. As previously stated, Aspies tend to dwell on events that have gone wrong in the past and set up self-fulfilling prophecies for those negative experiences to repeat themselves in the future. They ruminate about ways they wish they could change, ways they wish they could change others, and even ways they want to change the world. On a more mundane level, they often wish they had not said what they just said in an inconsequential conversation. These frequent "I wish" thoughts can turn obsessive and endlessly recycle themselves.

An example of this kind of obsessive thinking involves two individuals I know, both of whom are on the spectrum. After meeting Jane at a conference, Steve was interested in pursuing a relationship with her. At first Jane was fine with Steve's intentions, but after a couple of dates she wasn't interested in cultivating the relationship when it became clear that he was more serious about her than she was about him. Jane was no longer enjoying the time she spent with Steve and thought it best not to see him any more. She wrote him a friendly e-mail, suggesting that it was time they go their separate ways and she wished him well. Steve was very upset. He had invested too much in the relationship and felt hurt, betrayed, and confused. His reaction was clearly disproportionate to the circumstances. He and Jane had only gone out a couple of times and there had been no sexual involvement. Steve became depressed and blamed Jane for his despair. During the next six months, Steve spoke to his therapist, his minister, and a few friends but nothing made him feel any better.

Steve felt that Jane was his spiritual soul mate (despite their limited contact) and felt that she had ruined his life by terminating their relationship. He was not willing to abandon that viewpoint in order to accommodate a more realistic perspective. After six months he still couldn't let go of his obsession with Jane, even though it was causing him great despair.

For Steve's dark night to have any meaning or resolution, he would need to shift away from these obsessive thoughts to a more reality-based understanding. Although some neurotypicals could have a similar reaction to Steve, most people would have been sufficiently resilient to appreciate why Jane ended the relationship. As previously noted, Aspies tend to be black-and-white thinkers and will either overly blame themselves for screwing up a relationship or become angry with the other person for rejecting them. Seeing the "gray" in this situation—that neither he nor Jane was to blame—was not even an option for Steve. As long as he continues to obsess about Jane, his dark night could go on forever, and he will never gain the strength to move on from his disappointment. He will never learn the lesson that he can't control the way Jane, or anyone else, feels about him.

For people with Asperger's to move out of their dark nights, they have to ask themselves what lessons they need to learn to feel better about life. The first step in this process is being open to receiving help from others. This can be difficult for people with Asperger's who generally don't like asking for help. They don't want to appear weak or incompetent and requesting help forces them to take the initiative, something else they would prefer not to do.

If Aspies want to learn from their dark nights, another obstacle to confront is their resistance to change. Change involves stepping out of one's comfort zone and dealing with the unknown. No one knows exactly what will happen until an experience unfolds. This is difficult for many Aspies who like to know how things will turn out ahead of time so they can avoid making a mistake. They like to believe there is either a right or wrong way to proceed, and they should be able to know what the right choice is in advance. I know a young man with Asperger's who became angry at himself for making a mistake when he went on his first date. Because he had no prior dating experience, he decided to bring the date a bouquet of flowers. Later, some friends told him that bringing flowers on a first date was excessive and pathetic. He felt terrible about this mistake and thought it was something he should have known, even though he had no prior dating experience.

A wise person once said you can't know what you don't know yet. This simple truth explains why people with Asperger's often have trouble being open to feedback. Aspies are often resistant to input because it would threaten their inner critic's belief that they should already know what they don't know. This resistance typically presents itself as stubbornness or defensiveness and can keep one locked in the dark night a lot longer than necessary.

An illustration of this type of stubbornness came up one summer I when was going to Oxford, England, to take classes toward my master's degree. I didn't know what types of clothes to pack or how much money to bring, and lacked some other significant information about the trip. When my parents tried to discuss these issues with me, my defenses went up. I became belligerent and told them I didn't want to discuss anything. I totally shut down. Looking back on this incident, I realize that at the time I felt like a child who was unprepared to go overseas on a trip and didn't have any of the relevant information. I also could see that in order for me to get this information, I would have to take the initiative and ask someone for help. I would have to call the person in charge of the trip or a fellow student, neither of which I was willing to do. I dug in my heels in an effort to avoid feelings of inadequacy, which is a common defense mechanism for those with Asperger's.

Besides being open to the feedback of others, it is equally important to pay attention to one's inner wisdom. Instead of automatically dismissing what might be uncomfortable or challenging feelings, try to sit with them and give them some time to marinate. After a while, if something resonates, it could be the first step out of depression.

How does someone with Asperger's, or anyone for that matter, distinguish between feedback that has merit and input that should be rejected? The answer to that question depends on one's level of resistance. If an insight doesn't seem to fit or make sense, trust your gut. For example, if someone said to me, "You are so conceited," that comment would simply roll off my back. It would not resonate or make sense with anything I know about myself, so I would reject it and not get upset about it.

However, if a comment is made that evokes strong feelings, it is wise to pay attention to it. A strong response may be trying to shield you from an insight that might seem initially painful on the surface but once absorbed will help you begin your transformation. This was certainly the case with my combative reaction to my parents when they tried to discuss my trip to Oxford with me. I was extremely defensive and stubborn in my insistence not to deal with these trip issues. If I had been able to pay attention and sit with these feelings, I would have learned something new about myself that would have been helpful to me.

Carl Jung calls this process a "confrontation with the unconscious" (Moore 2004), in which one opens up to feedback from the entire psyche, including that of the inner child. If parts of your childhood were traumatic (as is the case for many Aspies), the part that was never allowed full expression may still be trying to break through into consciousness. The inner child is the part of you that is whole, creative, vibrant, and Aspergerian. It's the part of you that existed before your inner critic was ever allowed to say a word, the part that was originally innocent and pure before being socialized into a neurotypical world that probably began in nursery school and continues to this day. Allow the inner child to guide you during your dark night. Be open to its wisdom. If your inner child seems playful, silly, or even goofy, go with it. Perhaps it's trying to teach you to lighten up, go with the flow, not take your perceived challenges too seriously and remind you that life is transitory and provisional. Longchenpa, a very wise Buddhist in fourteenth-century Tibet, recognized that laughter and acceptance are better responses to depression than self-judgment. This paradoxical bit of wisdom is very good advice and worth remembering when the going gets rough.

Had I been able to listen and make sense of my response to my parents about the trip to Oxford, I would have seen it was my inner child defending against feeling incompetent and ill-equipped to go so far away from home. Had I been able to work with my response and figure out what it meant, I might have been on the road toward positive change, but I wasn't ready for that yet.

The process of self-investigation is not easy, especially when it involves examining adult issues like dating, employment, transitions, and self-care. People in your life may be telling you to grow up and to start acting your age. You may be feeling pressure to move out of the house, find a job, get married, and have kids. But these things may pose difficult challenges or may not represent your true needs. While the world is telling you to catch up to your age, your inner child may be shutting down to avoid feeling threatened and ashamed. As paradoxical as it seems, your inner child can be one of the best resources you have toward becoming an adult.

Being in touch with my inner child helped me make the transition from not understanding my differences to finally becoming open to the possibility that I actually was different. I had to embrace a concept that would have seemed unacceptable to me prior to that time—I was autistic. The only impediment I now had to overcome was to be open to a new way of viewing myself. My self-image had to be updated. Being in touch with my inner child helped me accept having Asperger's, I was able to be more honest with myself than in the past in assessing my strengths and weaknesses. I could even laugh at some of my differences, which gave me greater self-acceptance. Instead of denying my interests as I did when I was younger, I could now appreciate that my taste in music, television, movies, and books was not mainstream, but reflected my true interests. I stopped fighting who I was and engaged in more self-acceptance. Relying on the wisdom of your inner child may seem counterproductive, but nothing could be further from the truth. When I couldn't accept being different from others, it only served to silence the voice of my inner child.

I tried to bring an openness to being diagnosed with Asperger syndrome. Even though I initially felt some clarity in receiving this diagnosis, I still pictured living in my parents' basement for the rest of my life. I thought I would never be able to live on my own and that I had nothing to offer the world. This negative image scared me to death. It made me probe deeply into myself until I discovered a new perspective that turned out to be transformative. Being diagnosed with Asperger syndrome eventually became a liberating experience for me. It explained the events of my life in a way nothing previously had. It allowed me to advocate for myself in ways I couldn't have before, and it gave me a better self-image. It also provided me with an understanding of my differences that I could not only accept, but could also ultimately view as strengths.

Everyone's circumstances are different, and I'm not suggesting that someone's Asperger's diagnosis would be the positive, life-changing event it was for me. As I mentioned, my cousin Arthur, who has Asperger's, leads a very successful life but doesn't pay much attention to the diagnosis. But for me, it was the diagnosis that brought me out of the dark night of the soul. For so long, I had resisted the thought that I was different. As it turned out, this thought was exactly what I needed to accept about myself in order to move forward with my life. Carl Jung once said, "What you resist persists." If you find you are resisting something about yourself, there's probably a reason for it. Probe a little deeper and find out what that reason might be.

To take action is often as simple as accepting what is. In other words, accepting reality that one does not have the power to change. That may sound like a passive stance, but in reality it involves a lot of hard work. The humanistic psychotherapist Carl Rogers once said, "The curious paradox is that when I accept myself just as I am, then I can change" (Blaydes 2003). That statement was certainly true for me. The more I resisted my true nature, the further away I was from myself. When I began to accept myself, the insights I needed to clearly understand myself came to me rather effortlessly.

It is not only important to accept yourself, but also to accept whatever your current circumstances might be. Assume I am behind four games in a tennis match. If I start to dwell on the score, I will surely lose. However, if I take it one point at a time I may lose anyway, but at least I will give myself a fighting chance to win. I once did play a match where I was down 6–1, 5–2, and 40–love. Instead of focusing on the score or that I was losing so badly, I concentrated only on the point at hand and ended up winning the match.

But, as we all know, winning isn't everything. Some of my major losses in tennis have inspired me to become a better player. Pete Sampras attributes his 1992 U.S. Open loss in the finals to

Stefan Edberg as the match that ultimately sharpened his focus and eventually allowed him to become one of the greatest players of all time. As most successful people will tell you, they didn't get to where they are without learning from their share of failures. Before becoming co-host on NBC's *Today* show and head anchor for the *CBS Evening News*, Katie Couric was told by CNN that she had no talent. Michael Jordan was cut from his high school basketball team before being recognized as perhaps the greatest basketball player of all time.

Pause-and-Reflect Questions

Pause and reflect on these activities that may help you move forward during a dark night:

1. If exercise is not part of your life, begin making it a part of your daily routine. Exercise not only keeps your body from stagnating but your mind as well.

2. Meditation and prayer can be very important practices in helping you to regroup.

3. Psychotherapy and supportive people can help encourage you and provide insights that you may not be able to see.

4. Ask yourself what lessons you need to learn in order to grow from the dark night. The word "lesson" doesn't imply that you did something wrong and deserve blame, nor does it mean God is trying to teach you something. Rather, ask yourself what it is you're resisting that is evoking the most emotion from you. Chances are this is the area in which you need to begin your work.

5. Be open to change and, at the same time, accept what is. Be willing to let go of self-defeating schemas, attitudes, and actions.

There is no denying that having Asperger's provides many personal challenges, but it doesn't mean you have to be a victim. Remember that every setback can be a test of your level of resiliency. Keep in mind that whatever is happening in your life right now, this too shall pass.

Chapter 5

Suicide is the Forever Decision

This chapter is very personal for me. As I have shared, there have been times in my life when I've thought about suicide but I have never in any way acted on it. At those times it seemed death was a way to end the relentless pain. I know firsthand how seductive suicide can seem when one is in the midst of a bleak depression or a dark night.

Suicide attempts are commonly reported among individuals with Asperger syndrome (Gillberg 2002). Howlin (2005) reviewed 35 different studies and pointed out that depression and anxiety accounted for most of the psychiatric disturbances, including attempted suicide, among those with Asperger's.

If you have ever contemplated suicide, it is important to know that you have every right to feel this way, but I want to encourage you strongly to think about and ultimately decide to choose an alternative.

Throughout this book, I have challenged you to do two things: accept the circumstances of your life, and find ways to move toward constructive change. The process can't work in the reverse. Change can't happen before acceptance. Paradoxically, the more you yearn for change, the more it won't happen until you are able to accept your true self and your life's circumstances.

THE AUTISM SPECTRUM AND DEPRESSION

I understand wanting to end your life as a way to stop your suffering. You want the quality of your life to be different and less painful but you can't imagine that ever happening. You wish you were never born. These are understandable ways to feel when you are severely depressed, but the act of suicide produces irreversible results and tragic consequences that preclude any opportunity for real change.

If you have never had the opportunity to watch the classic film *It's a Wonderful Life*, I encourage you to see it. It's always on television around Christmas. Jimmy Stewart plays George Bailey, a self-sacrificing man who has always set aside his own ambitions for the good of others. After facing a false bank fraud charge, an impending arrest, and bankruptcy, George decides to get drunk and jump off a bridge into a river to end his life. Before he is able to accomplish this objective, he sees an old man jumping off the bridge, presumably to try to kill himself. Because George is self-sacrificing by nature, he jumps into the river to save the old man's life. Later he learns that this man is actually his guardian angel, Clarence.

Clarence's assignment is to help George see the difference he has made in the lives of others and give him a new perspective on his life. Clarence wants to be successful as George's guardian angel because it will finally get him into heaven where he will become an Angel First Class and get his wings. To prove to George that he is actually his guardian angel, Clarence decides to grant George's wish that he was never born. Clarence creates a reality in which George can observe what life would have been like without his presence on earth. As it turns out, the quality of life for those who knew George turns out to be a lot worse in this alternative scenario. Because George never existed, his wife is now an unhappy old maid, his uncle has been put into an insane asylum, his younger brother Harry has died at an early age, and even the town of Bedford Falls has a different name. No one even recognizes George because he was never born. As a result of seeing the positive impact he had on people's lives, George eventually comes to see that his life had meaning. George frantically returns to the river and begs Clarence for his help.

George discovers that he can no longer hear out of one ear and has a bloody lip. Tears of joy fill his eyes as he realizes he is back in reality. He feels a rush of gratitude for merely being alive. When he goes back to his home, he sees the police are at his house to take him to jail. However the townspeople have taken up a collection to save George and his family. This is when George truly becomes aware that despite all the problems he had, he did have a wonderful life, and he thanks Clarence for helping him come to that life-affirming realization.

I'm certainly no angel and don't have Clarence's powers, but I would like you to consider for a moment that your life has probably made more of a positive impact on other people than you realize. To illustrate my point, I want to share something that happened to me several years ago. I ran into an old high school classmate while I was at the grocery store. He was a popular jock and someone I would have thought never knew I existed in high school. To my surprise he not only remembered me, but he actually thanked me for not being afraid to be myself. He said that I gave other kids permission to be themselves. I was shocked. Throughout my high school years, I believed my existence was inconsequential, and it wouldn't have made any difference to anyone if I had lived or died.

This encounter made me wonder if the way I felt in high school is similar to the way other Aspies have felt about themselves: that they also flew under the radar, went unnoticed and were negatively judged by others. If that were true, then they too would be surprised to learn they had enhanced the lives of others in ways they might never have known.

These encounters brought some other people to mind. I read about a boy with Asperger's who went through a severe depression and wanted to die but months later went on to win his district spelling bee. Or the autistic young man I saw on all the news channels who, after sitting on the bench for his entire high school basketball career, scored six three-point baskets in a row in the final game of his senior year. And the man with Asperger's who wrote an article about running into an old middle school classmate who thanked him profusely for standing up to a bully on his behalf.

I believe people on the autism spectrum are here for a specific reason. Although each of us has his or her own individual goals in life, as a group we can collectively help accelerate the process of teaching people to accept others with differences. Our purpose involves holding up a mirror to others so they can see *everyone* has insecurities stemming from being or feeling different. The more open and accepting we can be about our differences, the more other people can learn from our example and accept themselves. If we can model that differences don't need to be hidden or be a cause for shame, people will take notice and become more compassionate toward others as well as themselves.

Along with modeling self-acceptance, there are other traits those with Asperger's can be proud of, such as the willingness to tell the truth even when it is uncomfortable to do so, our dogged determination to finish what we start, and the passion we devote to our special interests. I believe the lives of neurotypicals can be enriched by the presence of those on the spectrum.

The Risk

There is a huge risk in trying to commit suicide. If you are unsuccessful, you may have to live out the rest of your life in a wheelchair, brain damaged, blind, or with other irreversible and permanent physical and mental conditions. There is no sure-fire way to kill yourself. Some people have even survived jumping off the Golden Gate Bridge in San Francisco and many have aimed a gun at themselves and failed to hit the intended vital organ. Is it really worth the risk of becoming permanently incapacitated? Think about how high the stakes are. No matter how much pain you may be going through now, nothing could possibly be worth the pain that could await you if your suicide is unsuccessful. And if you are successful, the pain you are inflicting on your loved ones is incalculable.

Steps to Take When You are Feeling Suicidal

The most important thing to do is to get rid of any firearms or sharp knives in your possession. If there are firearms or sharp knives in the place where you live, ask your parents, siblings or the person in control of the weapons either to remove them or place them somewhere where you won't have access to them.

Also assess how much energy you have. If you are just starting to recover from a severe episode of depression, this is actually a time when a suicide attempt is more likely to occur. During the height of a depressive episode, there is usually not enough energy to carry out an attempt even if someone wanted to do so. However, when coming out of an episode, the feeling of not wanting to live may still be present, and there might be a sufficient increase in energy to carry through with the plan. This is especially true with bipolar depression. Try not to be alone when rebounding from a severe episode. Go to your parents' or a friend's home and get immediate help from a therapist. If need be, call a suicide or crisis hotline and consider seeking inpatient treatment. Recognizing the threat of suicide and taking these suggested steps is an attempt to buy time so that those feelings can pass. Don't hesitate to tell people how you are feeling and don't worry about being judged or appearing weak. This is a time to put aside pride and get the necessary help you need.

Also, if family members or friends do not know exactly what to say to you at this time, understand that they are scared of losing you and they are trying their best. In some ways it is preferable to talk to a professional who can be nonreactive, yet caring and compassionate. Professionals are legally obligated to hospitalize you for a period of time if you say you intend to kill yourself and have a plan. However, this action will only happen if you refuse to agree that you won't kill yourself in between sessions. You cannot be hospitalized just for feeling suicidal and expressing those thoughts.

The saying "Suicide is a permanent solution to a temporary problem" is quite true. Feelings and situations in life are ephemeral. Even life itself is for a limited period of time. What someone is feeling today is not what that person will be feeling a year, five years, or even ten years from now. Feeling states are like weather conditions. Often, sunny skies come after the worst storms.

A man my father knew was down on his luck and had been out of work for more than five years. His wife had left him, and he felt that living was just too painful. Several people—my father included—encouraged him to hang on and be open to the fact that his life's circumstances could change. A few months later, he got a great job offer, eventually remarried, and is happier now than he ever was. But what if he had committed suicide during that time when everything looked so bleak and hopeless? He would never have known what was waiting for him.

No one should negatively judge another person for thinking about committing suicide. There is no way to understand the pain someone else is going through during a period of depression. Perhaps one of your parents has died, you've been unemployed for a while, or someone has ended a friendship with you. Whatever the situation, you want the suffering to come to an end, but the act of taking one's life cuts short infinite possibilities that will never have a chance to unfold. The people in your life who love you will doubtlessly go through an endless grieving process, and you will be in no position to console them in their grief when it occurs. You will not be able to tell them, "It's not your fault," even if you write it in a suicide note. They will always wonder whether they could have done more. That is why I will do everything in my power to persuade a person from not taking that final act. Eventually we will all die. Someday we will all be gone from this earth, with or without our direct actions. However, while we are still here, we might as well enjoy the ride. James Taylor put this phrase to music: "The secret of life is enjoying the passage of time. Any fool can do it, there ain't nothing to it." Life is like a book, and you only know the story up to the page you are on right now. You can't flip to the last page. Unless you keep reading, there is no way to know what will happen on the next page, in the following chapter, or how the book will ultimately end. You have to keep reading to see how the story unfolds.

Chapter 6

Perfectionism and Depression

People with Asperger syndrome are, by nature, perfectionists. This means that their lives will have an excessive amount of anxiety and depression. Wanting to be perfect is a natural human impulse. Many religions, particularly Christianity, believe that people should strive for God's perfection, but there is a catch. That Jesus died for man's sins makes it possible for us to sin by not being perfect and, yet, still be forgiven. One of the reasons the experience of being "born again" is so emotionally powerful is because people suddenly feel cleansed of their imperfections. Earlier, I talked about why conversion experiences often take place in prison, on deathbeds, and after hitting rock bottom in life. To be forgiven by a higher power that supposedly knows the nature of all of our misdeeds, whether large or small, is a transforming experience because it speaks to a kind of love everyone would like to have in their lives.

Although I am not Christian, I can understand why Christianity promotes the notion of personal forgiveness among its believers. The theme of forgiveness is a dynamic way of encouraging positive change in people's lives. As long as we are human, however, we are going to be imperfect. Instead of needing to forgive ourselves for being less than perfect, it makes more sense to accept and even embrace that fact. Alcoholics Anonymous uses this philosophy as the blueprint for its successful 12-step program.

Andre Agassi was one of the world's best tennis players. In *Open: An Autobiography* (2009), he recounts that he had a breakthrough in his game when a new coach told him not to worry about playing each point perfectly. Once he could accept the fallacy of trying to achieve perfection, his game significantly improved.

In *The Spirituality of Imperfection: Storytelling and the Search for Meaning*, Kurtz and Ketcham (1993) refer to the pursuit of perfection as humanity's most tragic mistake. An example of this pursuit dramatically gone awry is that of Adolf Hitler, who aimed for utopian perfection by trying to purify and cleanse the Aryan race by eliminating millions of Jews, Gypsies, homosexuals, and others who he felt were contaminants. The end result was destruction on a grand scale and, ultimately, Hitler's own self-destruction.

Kurtz and Ketcham quote the Zen master Shunryu Suzuki, who said, "The goal of practice is always to keep the beginner's mind. The beginner's mind is always ready for anything; it is open to everything. In the beginner's mind there are many possibilities; in the expert's mind there are few" (p.141). What Suzuzki says is not just a metaphor. It is reality. Being human makes us all fallible one way or the other.

As Dr. Tony Attwood (2008) notes in his acclaimed book, *The Complete Guide to Asperger's Syndrome*, people with AS are very adept at noticing their mistakes and have a great fear of failure. He also notes that they tend to abandon projects if they don't have immediate success. They tend to finish things at which they are good but rarely attempt projects for which they have little aptitude. Speaking from personal experience, I have been a perfectionist most of my life, and much of the perfectionism has stemmed from caring too much about what other people think of me.

I have worked very hard on this issue and have made a lot of progress. In the past, I would become very anxious about every little mistake I thought I might have made. I constantly worried about saying the wrong thing and possibly offending someone. These concerns totally colored my interactions with others. I was always worried about saying the wrong thing and would often convince myself that I did, even when that wasn't the case. I'd come home and browbeat myself for hours, replaying each interaction as if there was a DVD player in my head. Today, I find it ironic that I held myself to standards of perfection in areas that did not come naturally to me. How could I expect to be a smooth operator when socializing is an inherent weakness for me? I was holding myself to highly unrealistic standards.

Socializing is not the only area in which I held myself to impossibly high standards. I did so in practically every aspect of my life. If I took a test and got a 96 percent, I wasn't satisfied because it wasn't 100 percent. If I gave a presentation in which I stuttered a couple of times, I focused on the stuttering instead of the success of the overall speech. If I played a tennis match in which I won 6–0, 6 2, I'd be unhappy that I even dropped two games. Clearly, my inner critic was alive and well.

Why is it that Aspies are so concerned about being perfect? According to Alfred Adler, the father of individual psychology, all human beings experience a certain amount of inferiority. However, many individuals on the spectrum tend to cover up these feelings of inferiority by striving for perfection in other areas (Ansbacher and Ansbacher 1964). This is called compensating.

When I was in high school, the only part of my life that contributed to my self-esteem was being a good tennis player. Every time I lost a match, it shattered my sense of identity. In my mind, I wasn't good at doing anything. I wanted people to see that I excelled at something. When I stepped onto the tennis court, it was like I was being transformed into a different human being. I became so infused with a sense of competition that I literally saw my opponent as the enemy. Tennis became a way of redefining myself, but in doing so I placed enormous pressure on myself. My thinking at the time was, if I couldn't play tennis perfectly, then why play it at all? Of course now I can see how illogical that was. Instead of being able to enjoy the experience of competing against high-level players and being grateful for having the skills to play at that level, I took the opportunity to feel bad whenever I lost a match, a game, or even a point.

This same principle may also be why some people with Asperger's tend to dominate conversations with topics that only interest them. Doing this helps to compensate for the discomfort associated with their awkwardness in socializing. The subtext of this behavior is, "As long as I can keep control of the conversation, maybe the other person will think that I'm really smart and won't notice my social unease."

Ironically, trying to be perfect actually lowers one's self-esteem. If you have high self-esteem, you don't need to prove yourself to anyone, including yourself. People with high self-esteem tend to define themselves based on who they are as people rather than their accomplishments. As long as your accomplishments define and hold you to impossible standards, you will continue to be plagued with self-doubt, shame, and worry.

There are other reasons why people with Asperger's tend to be perfectionists. One is an overly developed sense of responsibility and integrity. If I am five minutes late to a meeting because I was caught in traffic, I might still berate myself for not having left earlier. Or perhaps I tell a white lie to spare someone's feelings but then feel guilty for days about my act of dishonesty.

It has been my experience that individuals with Asperger's tend to compare themselves negatively to other people, particularly those who are the most like them. I've met a number of people with Asperger's who think that because they can't perform savant-like calculations or don't have genius level IQs, they are totally worthless. It's very easy to get caught up in this way of thinking, especially when you are comparing yourself to other people who are "disabled" like you are. One can easily come to the conclusion that so-and-so has a disability, and even he can do things better than I can.

I used to compare myself with those on the spectrum who are married and have families. Every time I heard that one of my peers had settled down and found a mate, I felt happy for them and also somewhat envious. The fact that they were able to navigate the world of dating and ultimately be successful struck a chord of jealousy in me. Although one can never know the future, at this point in my life, being married and having children does not appeal to me. Now that

I have begun to accept who I am and what I really want, I am much less likely to compare myself to others.

Procrastination is another manifestation of perfectionism. Putting off doing something ensures that mistakes will not be made. Aspies often turn papers in late because they are working feverishly until the eleventh hour to make sure they are perfect. Also common for those with Asperger's is not taking on challenges unless they believe they will be successful. This unwillingness to risk failure limits their opportunities to participate in activities that may enhance the quality of their lives. If, for example, someone invited me to play a game of pool, I'd probably decline the invitation. The only way I would consider it is if I hired someone to teach me some pool skills first. As is true with many Aspies, being vulnerable at any activity only accentuates inherent feelings of differentness.

Being a perfectionist creates a major drawback in living a fulfilling life. A perfectionist has to be extremely cautious. If you have difficulty participating in activities where you might not do well, you will be erring on the side of caution and keeping yourself from living the most fulfilling life possible.

One way of becoming desensitized to perfectionism would be to try something you know you don't do well. Let's say bowling isn't an activity at which you have excelled. You might go by yourself and bowl a game or two. Experience how it feels to be uncoordinated and unsuccessful while engaging in a new activity. Perhaps you fear appearing foolish to others. If you try enough things that you might not be good at, you'll get to the point where you will desensitize yourself to the fear of failure and not care so much about what others think. You will also find that you can become better at doing certain things you never thought possible. You'll see the world won't come to an end if people see you performing a particular task poorly. Others will notice that you can enjoy yourself without having to be perfect at what you are doing.

I don't consider myself to be a funny person. There used to be a time when I would be jealous of someone who could tell jokes, even if they weren't funny. Sometimes I would try to emulate these people and my jokes would bomb. Finally I reached a point of frustration and simply stopped trying to interject humor into any conversation. My thought was that if I couldn't be really funny, it was pointless to try. My ego couldn't handle the fact that other people could tell jokes better than me. As a defense mechanism, I stopped trying to compete with them. In reality, it wasn't a competition at all. Certain people are just funnier than others, which is something I can now accept without a loss of self-esteem. Holding myself to such an unrealistic standard and then retreating when I didn't meet that standard made me withdraw in a number of situations where I doubted my ability to be successful. And that seems to be the pattern with many people on the spectrum: "If I can't do something perfectly, why should I do it all?" Fortunately, I have now gotten to the point where I am comfortable telling a joke and not having a room full of people fall down in hysterics. My sense of self is strong enough that I can feel good about who I am and not judge myself based on how funny I am compared to others. When I'm not funny, my reaction now is more along the lines of "Oh well. You win some, you lose some."

Fear of rejection is another aspect of perfectionism. My mother is a playwright who has had many of her plays produced at theaters around the country. For every 50 plays she submits to theaters, she may only get one response back. She also has to deal with critics who review her plays in the newspaper once they have opened. She has received everything from rave reviews to very poor notices and everything in between. Like all artists, she never knows ahead of time how audiences or critics will receive her plays. She just has to put her work and herself out there and see what happens. It's scary but it's a necessary part of the process. Like writers who have to deal with their share of rejection, we all have to toughen our skins a little so that we don't limit ourselves in life.

Freeing yourself from being a perfectionist will admittedly be very challenging. It might help to repeat these affirmations daily:

- I am who I am and not what I do.

- Nobody's opinion of me matters more than my own.

- My self-worth is based on my good qualities and not on my talents.

- I can do something even if I'm not perfect at it. As a matter of fact, I could do something and be utterly lousy at it and still have fun.

This chapter speaks to the heart of how we tend to devalue ourselves as human beings for illegitimate reasons. Breaking the habit of needing to be perfect all of the time will do wonders for your self-esteem and help to keep symptoms of depression under control. All of us live in a challenging world. Why make it even harder on yourself than you need to? Relish your imperfections in the same way you celebrate what you're good at. Try your best and feel good about your effort.

Pause-and-Reflect Questions

1. In what ways does perfectionism limit you?

2. What is an activity you would be willing to try even if you are not good at it?

Chapter 7

Anger and Depression

Anger can be a useful and constructive emotion when it is expressed in a healthy way. Many people with Asperger's have put their anger to good use. Aspies tend to speak out about injustice. Children with AS are frequently referred to as the "little policeman" of the playground because of their contempt for bullying and their willingness to report it.

When anger is expressed assertively and without aggression, it is empowering. Unfortunately most of us express anger in ways that are disempowering. It is very hard for people, whether neurotypical or on the spectrum, to admit when they are wrong. When involved in some kind of conflict, it is natural to want the other person to say "I'm sorry," but that may not happen. For those with Asperger's, not getting an apology for a perceived wrong can be particularly hurtful. They need the other person to see that they were right and apologize to them.

Aspies are especially frustrated when others do not try to understand their point of view. When others don't understand them, Aspies are quick to become hurt because they think their feelings aren't being taken seriously. Their hurt quickly turns to anger, and then they are hurt again by not receiving the apology they need. Unfortunately the end result is they are the ones who end up paying the price for needing to be right.

Dr. Tony Attwood discusses anger at length in *The Complete Guide to Asperger's Syndrome* (2008). He stresses the fact that many people with Asperger's have a difficult time identifying and labeling their own emotions. He goes on to say that they tend to express anger in place of sadness and experience immediate physical reactions to people and events even before they've had a chance to process their thoughts. Think of a car that can go from 0 to 60 miles an hour in a matter of seconds. The same thing is true for a person with Asperger's who can go from calm to angry to rage in a very short amount of time. Attwood identifies the culprit as an overactive amygdala, which is part of the limbic system in the brain. He compares the amygdala to the dashboard of a car that enables the driver to maintain an equilibrium on the road as well as provide any warning signs that the car is about to break down. The frontal lobes of the brain are the equivalent of the driver who makes the decisions on behalf of the car. However, with Asperger's, the dashboard causes inconsistent readings to occur. The amygdala alerts the driver that the engine is about to break down when perhaps the odometer simply needs minor adjusting. The important point to remember is there is a physiological reason why people with Asperger's become so worked up over incidents that might not fluster other people.

Attwood also says that anger can sometimes act as a mask for depression. As a clinician, Attwood noticed that many individuals who are clinically depressed tend to externalize their feelings of worthlessness, shame, guilt, and low self-esteem through the expression of anger. This is not surprising because men (more so than women) tend to externalize negative emotions through destructive behavior. This observation takes on increasing importance given that the majority of those with Asperger's are male.

Externalizing negative emotions can happen in one of two ways: either through behaviors like physical abuse, verbal abuse, addiction to alcohol, drugs, gambling, and food, or through the use of thought projections.

Projecting a thought onto another person means taking a negative thought about oneself and pushing it out of consciousness by superimposing it on another person. For example, if I am angry at a friend but have trouble dealing with it, I might project the anger onto him and say, "What's wrong with you? Why are you angry with me?" That process eliminates the need to cope with that unpleasant feeling by making it someone else's problem.

Blaming others for one's own feelings is often easier than owning the feelings. This is often why people tend to dislike other people who share similar negative traits. They unconsciously recognize qualities in others that they dislike in themselves.

Perfectionism can also lead to anger. I noted earlier that people with Asperger's tend to be hypercritical of themselves. When this perfectionism is externalized against family, friends, and co-workers, anger is bound to occur. I am aware of my tendency to be critical of other people. Sometimes I hold others to my own standards of perfection. For example, I am never late. Punctuality is extremely important to me, so if another person is a few minutes late to a meeting with me, it can throw me into a tailspin and stimulate anger.

A number of years ago a friend stopped by my apartment unannounced. This unplanned visit caused me to get upset. From her point of view I was acting totally irrationally. From my point of view, I would never show up at someone's place without calling first. It is these types of communicational misunderstandings that can cause rifts between people with Asperger's and their neurotypical friends and loved ones.

Thought projections are tricky business. Whenever you are being judgmental or critical, try to determine if you are projecting your own feelings onto someone else. An example could be my thoughts about the garbage man. If I see the garbage man as a loser because he should be capable of accomplishing more with his life, I would be judging him by the standards I apply to myself. That thought would have nothing to do with him and everything to do with me. The garbage man could be very happy and gratified with his occupation. He is providing for his family and serving an important purpose for the community. I would be projecting my own dissatisfaction if I had to collect garbage.

Quick to Anger

The most important thing to do when triggered by anger is to slow down. The worst thing to do is act on anger when it's at its peak. People are never their most rational when they are in a reactive state. Being in the midst of a blind rage is not the time to draw conclusions or to make any decisions. Unfortunately, these are often the times when people feel compelled to act and wind up regretting it. This is especially true for those with Asperger's, who often act while they are feeling angry. Think about all the times you have written a nasty e-mail, left an angry voicemail message, or said something you wish you could take back. Chances are these responses happened when your anger reached the point where you could not calmly assess the situation. This doesn't mean that if you waited, your anger would necessarily go away the next day or even the next week. It means that you are giving yourself an opportunity to reflect on the situation in a calmer state of mind. By waiting until you have calmed down a little, you won't let your anger dictate your response, and you will be able to make a more rational choice about what to do.

The Need to be Right

It is an unfortunate human trait that most people feel the need to be right. If the human race is not careful, this trait could cause the downfall of humanity. Because of excessive pride, close friendships end, nations go to war, marriages break up, and lawsuits proliferate. When someone is angry, nothing is more important than being right. Two angry people or two warring nations will rarely come to any sort of mutual understanding when they are both dogmatic and unyielding.

Anger leads to depression when conflicts cannot be resolved and disputes cannot be settled. How to avoid this fate? It is crucial to remember that people are more receptive to feedback or criticism when they're not feeling attacked. To accomplish this objective, the person who is angry needs the ability to calm down and wait until equilibrium is restored. But even being conscious enough to withhold reactivity doesn't guarantee that others will always agree with you. In this respect, interpersonal conflict is very challenging for people with Asperger's because anger does not typically abate until the other person sees and agrees with their point of view.

When there is a legitimate need to communicate anger, the goal should always be to express it in a way that allows the other person to hear what you have to say. Do not use it as an opportunity to vent your feelings. Some strategies to make this process less contentious are to wait until you have calmed down and choose a time when you and the other person can resolve the matter without being rushed. Also, be careful of your tone of voice and the words that you use. Stay away from words like "always" and "never" and keep the feelings focused on only one incident rather than bringing up events from the past. Avoid generalizations and global statements. Use "I" versus "you" messages. It's preferable to say, "I felt inconvenienced and upset when you were an hour late," as opposed to, "What a jerk! You're always late. Don't you ever think about anyone else's feelings but your own?" How you express anger is just as important as the content.

There comes a time in everyone's life when maturity sets in and with it a realization that battles have to be chosen carefully. Sometimes being right is very important; other times it's not. If I was supposed to meet a friend for dinner and she thought it was at 6 p.m. but I thought it was at 7 p.m., it's not that important who made the mistake. These kinds of situations are difficult for Aspies because of their need to have the other person admit fault. In the mind of someone with Asperger's, the apology vindicates the Aspie and shows it wasn't his or her fault. Needing to be right over trivial matters creates unnecessary conflict. Next time you find yourself getting angry, ask yourself if the conflict is worth the potential risk of creating tension and resentment. Sometimes people simply need to be given the benefit of the doubt, especially when they have a proven track record. Not being able to let go of anger will inevitably contribute to depression as well as limit those who would want to have a friendship with you in the future.

THE AUTISM SPECTRUM AND DEPRESSION

Other People's Lies

I can hear some readers saying, "Hey, what's trivial to you might not be so trivial to me." And this is true. For example, telling a white lie is usually not a big deal and doesn't usually warrant an angry response. But for many with Asperger's, it is a very big deal because when people lie (even about small matters), it makes them feel less safe in an already unsafe world. If Aspies can't trust the people who love them to tell the truth 100 percent of the time, whom can they trust?

When this kind of automatic, angry response occurs, a cognitive reframing is necessary. Try to remember that most people who lie usually don't have malicious intentions. Perhaps they are embarrassed about something and are trying to cover their tracks. Or maybe they don't want to cause hurt feelings or aren't even aware of having lied. Those kinds of white lies need to be separated from lies that can create real mistrust. Some lies really do compromise the integrity of a relationship, such as infidelity.

Letting Go

Several years ago, I spoke to a man in his mid 20s with Asperger's, who was still angry at his kindergarten teacher for holding him back a year and forcing him to repeat that grade. Even though 20 years had elapsed, it bothered him so much that he wanted to write a letter to this teacher letting her know the effect her decision had on his life. He asked me whether I thought writing this letter was a healthy act on his part. I told him that I thought it was good idea only if it brought him a sense of closure. I warned him against the dangers of expecting an apology or some kind of reconciliation that might not come to pass. I also suggested he could write the letter that would enable him to let go of his feelings, and then decide whether or to not send it.

It is common for people with Asperger's to be angry at the system for causing them to experience failure. I met a lawyer with Asperger's who talked bitterly about how there are no opportunities in the legal community for people like her. She felt that because of the difficulties she had in giving a good interview, various law firms were discriminating against her simply because she was an Aspie. A more rational way to view her dilemma is that any person who gives a bad interview may have difficulty getting a job. She needed to focus on improving her interviewing skills and not on being a victim.

It seems there are many legitimate reasons for people who are on the spectrum to be angry. Whether the source of this anger is legitimate or not is irrelevant. The important point is to see how anger can contribute to depression. Anger often acts as a buffer for sadness. The more we blame others for our hardships in life, the more power we give them and the less responsibility we take in assuming that power for ourselves. It is ironic that the very people we are the angriest with are the people to whom we give the most power.

Think of it this way: when people are angry, they are less in charge of their lives. The people with whom they are angry have tremendous control over them. If they could release their anger, these people would become less significant to them. This kind of release is why some families of murder victims (some of whom probably wanted to kill the murderer at one point) eventually forgave or are involved in the process of letting go of their anger toward the murderer. They don't let go of the anger for the murderer's sake, but rather because they don't want to give the murderer even more power than he already has in taking away a beloved family member.

Letting go of anger toward people and institutions is not an easy process, but there is a big payoff. You will no longer be drained of the energy it takes to maintain that anger. If your anger has reached the place where you can't forgive others who you feel have wronged you, talk it over with a therapist. Let a professional help you process whatever hurt and pain you are experiencing. The end goal should always be to move away from the grip anger has on you.

Releasing anger that was previously directed toward someone can be as simple as saying to yourself, "I refuse to let you continue to drain me of the energy I need to live productively. You aren't important enough for me to make that kind of sacrifice any more. I hereby release my anger toward you." Saying or writing this declaration may seem a bit contrived, but if you repeat it, pretty soon the words will begin to take on meaning and you will start to believe the value behind this message. When you begin to see how anger negatively affects you, holding on to it will seem far less appealing.

The less anger you have accumulated from past events in your life, the more energy you will have to deal with the root cause of your depression. Being angry acts as a buffer for dealing with pain because it's a lot easier to be angry with others than it is to take responsibility for your own inner turmoil. As long as you are angry, you don't have to face those inner demons because your attention is self-righteously focused outward.

There is also a secondary gain to releasing previously directed anger toward others. You may begin to experience other feelings that have been repressed by the anger, such as sadness or self-loathing. Anger can keep a person stuck in the past or fixated on the future. Being angry with people or events from the past is futile because the past can't be changed. You need to come to terms with the fact that some of the injustices you have experienced will never be rectified. Some of the people who owe you apologies will never come forward. In coming to terms with anger from the past, you have choices to make. You can let past anger make you feel victimized and depressed, or you can empower yourself by letting go and moving forward. You can maintain a cynical attitude that everyone you meet will be like those who hurt you in the past, or you can approach each new person in your life with fresh eyes. I invite you to try the latter and see what results it produces in your life.

Pause-and-Reflect Questions

1. How you do you generally deal with anger?

2. How can you improve the way you tend to express your angry feelings?

Chapter 8

Managing Depression

The emphasis in this chapter is on different depression management strategies as well as areas that frequently trigger depression for people with Asperger's. While much of this book has been focused on the causes, types, and manifestations of depression, now it is time to look at some tangible steps to take to deal with it.

Medication

One of the questions I am asked most frequently by adults on the spectrum and their parents is whether medication is necessary or even a desirable option in the treatment and management of depression. This is obviously a very personal decision. Some people have to try several individual antidepressants or many different combinations of medication before finding the right formula. What makes prescribing drugs for depression so tricky is that each person responds differently to each medication. Whereas some medications work perfectly for some, they may cause terrible side effects in others.

I have been on antidepressants for over 15 years. They have been invaluable for me. Yet it took me about four or five different trials before I found the right combination to meet my needs. With some drugs, I had terrible side effects while others had no effect on me whatsoever. But once I found the right combination, I felt more stabilized, focused and less depressed. Antidepressants and anti-anxiety medications do work but they are not panaceas. They will not "cure" you of your depression. Unless you are willing to take some initiative and try some of the strategies recommended in this book and others, you'll find antidepressants minimally effective. When you use these powerful medications in conjunction with self-help, therapy, and other treatment approaches, antidepressants can be extremely helpful. Keep in mind that some medications take a few weeks to a month to start "kicking in" and most medications become progressively less effective over years and years of usage.

It is probable that the doctor whom you go to see for your yearly physicals and when you get sick can prescribe these medications. However, this is not the best alternative for a couple of reasons. Internists are not as well informed about the latest literature on these medications as psychiatrists are and they are even less knowledgeable about how Asperger syndrome can contribute to depression. Therefore, I would strongly recommend that you find a psychiatrist who specializes in or has some knowledge about adults on the autism spectrum. This may take some legwork on your part but your mental health is on the line if you opt for expediency. I once let my internist prescribe my antidepressants and it was a bad decision in many respects. He asked very few questions about my actual depression, no questions regarding my Asperger's, and I ended up with a combination that literally made me ill and it took months to wean me off them.

Some people with Asperger's are against taking medication because they view it as a sign of weakness. This position mistakenly assumes that depression is someone's "fault." As a matter of fact, many men have difficulties in even admitting that they suffer from depression because of the perceived lack of masculinity that is associated with depression in our culture. It is understandable why many people believe that depression is their fault but this is really a mistaken belief. It is also mistaken to view needing medication as a sign of weakness. Strong people ask for help, weak people worry too much about their self-image to do so. Asking for help doesn't necessarily mean taking medication, if you have a strong preference not to. It can mean making an appointment with a therapist, going to a depression or Asperger support group, or confiding in a good friend. However you choose to manage your depression, you will need to take some initiative and be proactive in the process. Whether you decide to try medication, join an online support group for Aspies, try psychotherapy, or confide in a close friend, it is important that you view these acts as being what they truly are: assertive and brave!

Mindfulness

One practice that reduces depressive symptoms and costs nothing is mindfulness. It is a wonderful technique that refers to being acutely aware of one's physical sensations by learning how to turn off the mental chatter in our heads: in other words, being in the moment without regard to past or future fears or concerns. Mindfulness is known as the seventh element of the Eightfold Path of Liberation in Buddhism. To be mindful is to be essentially merged with the moment in effortless awareness of one's environment.

Recent research has shown that mindfulness training can alter the neural expression of sadness (Farb *et al.* 2010) into a more content mental state. Mindfulness does not require assuming the lotus position and meditating. It simply means being present, which can be achieved through many different activities. It would be very difficult to worry about the next car payment or be depressed about something you did last week when playing a vigorous game of tennis, walking your dog, or reading an engrossing book. Being present can be accomplished through meditation as well as bringing a mindful attitude to the activities of the day. The practice of clearing one's mind helps to curtail the endless dialogue in our heads and allows us to bask in the clarity of silence.

Music

Since receiving an Asperger's diagnosis ten years ago, I've met hundreds of people with autism and almost all of them love music. In fact, most people on the spectrum are incredibly passionate about the importance of music in their lives. Music nourishes the soul and is the universal language of the spirit. Almost everyone can identify with music to one degree or another. It is the soundtrack that underscores the ebb and flow of our lives. It soothes us and its influence crosses all ethic, racial, religious, sexual, political, and geographical boundaries.

Research indicates that music helps to reduce suffering from depression and physical pain. Preliminary findings in a 2008 article in *The New York Times* suggested that when music therapy was analyzed for its effectiveness, it was considerably more successful than therapies that did not incorporate music, including talk therapy (see Parker-Pope 2008). In his well-known book *The Mozart Effect*, Don Campbell (1997) cites French auditory specialist Dr. Guy Berard, who noticed that when he gave his depressed patients a hearing profile called an audiogram, these patients were hypersensitive to certain frequencies while they were usually less sensitive to other frequencies. The frequencies to which depressed patients were sensitive exceeded well below or well above typical human sensitivity levels. Depressed patients displayed hypersensitivities to sound below 2000 hertz and above 8000 hertz and Berard found that the steeper this 2–8 curve became, the more likely the depressed person was to be suicidal. On the other hand, the non-depressed patients displayed more sensitivity in the normal range, between 2000 and 8000 hertz. In his book *Hearing Equals Behavior* (Berard and Brockett 2000), Berard claimed a 93 percent success rate in treating his patients for depression using music therapy.

People with chronic pain who listen to music will also be likely to reduce their intense symptoms by between 21 and 25 percent according to a 2006 controlled clinical trial in the *Journal of Advanced Nursing* (Blackwell Publishing Ltd. 2006).

Music helps trigger the release of dopamine, the neurotransmitter for pleasurable feelings (Levitin 2007). The famous philosopher John

Stuart Mill was routinely plagued by overwhelming depression and, reportedly, only music would give him a feeling of pleasure during those episodes (Sacks 2008). The famous writer William Styron commented in his memoir on depression that music pierced his heart like nothing else could, especially when he was close to committing suicide (Styron 1990).

My friend, Katie, who was the principal of a school for autistic children, once described a situation regarding a nine-year-old student. He had severe meltdowns in the classroom to the point where he often needed to be physically restrained by his teacher. Sometimes he would injure himself so badly he would have to be taken home. However, during lunchtime when the teacher would play Mozart on the stereo, his body would significantly relax. Watching this child, Katie had the distinct impression the music was speaking to him in a very powerful way.

The same thing was true for me as a child. There is a home video my father took in which I am jumping up and down and flapping my hands. While I was doing this, my dad put on the song from the musical *Annie* called "Tomorrow" and a sensation came over me similar to what I observed in the nine-year-old. All of a sudden, my body became perfectly still and my head turned toward the direction of the music. My ears became hyper-attuned to the sound coming from the stereo, and I had a look of joy in my eyes. Music therapist, professor, and fellow autistic Dr. Stephen Shore (2013) states that for severely autistic children, music can sometimes be the only means of communication with them.

Even at an early age, music was always the one thing that was sure to get my interest. I distinctly remember my father taking me to see Ray Charles, the show *Beatlemania*, and the Montreaux Jazz Festival in Detroit. Thinking about these musical events brings back wonderful memories for me.

Music was a saving grace throughout most of my childhood, adolescence, and young adulthood. It is the one therapeutic resource I consistently turn to for purposes of relaxation and is my form of meditation. Music speaks to me on a deeper level than other forms of communication, whether verbal or written. When I would come home from middle school after having been bullied and harassed, I'd put on a record by jazz pianist Erroll Garner, and his joyfully infused playing conveyed a message of hope and love. In essence his music was telling me, "Everything is going to be fine. Don't give up. There are better days ahead." Today when I listen to the music of Chopin, I feel like I'm hearing an outpouring of emotion from a man who definitely knew what it was like to have gone through the dark night of the soul and come back from it. His music suggests the tragedies in life and also the strength that can be attained by transcending adversity. When I hear a Beethoven symphony, I think of the misunderstood warrior emerging triumphant. No other language, philosophy, book, or religion can communicate these messages as clearly as the music of these masters.

Almost every autistic person I have ever met cites music as a primary special interest. I have talked to many different people at autism conferences and the conversation often turns to music. One man knew every doo-wop recording from the 1950s. Another was an expert on the Grand Ole Opry and could tell you about any performer who has played there during the past two decades. Yet another was an expert on music in general and is a virtual encyclopedia when it comes to every type of genre that has ever existed. He is impossible to beat in a game of musical trivia.

If music is already a part of your life, you don't need me to tell you that it can help when you are feeling depressed. But here are some suggestions that may increase the positive benefits music can have for you.

Try to listen to music in a room that you don't associate with stress. The idea is to pair your music with an environment that is as relaxing as possible so you begin to associate music with a peaceful and safe place. If your bedroom is where you are the least stressed, use this room as the place to get your daily quota of music. My bedroom is like a sanctuary; when my iPod stereo is on, I feel like I am recharging my body through the positive energy the music provides.

If driving is stressful for you, especially commuting to and from work, then listening to music in the car won't give you the same benefit you might get as in the bedroom. That is not to say you shouldn't listen to music in the car, but just don't designate it as part of your music therapy for the day. When you listen to music, it should be a full mind–body experience.

This brings me to my next point: musical balancing and counterbalancing. The following is a news bite I wrote for the *Autism Asperger's Digest* (September–October 2009) entitled "Music and Moods."

It is said that music is the universal language of the spirit. Music can lull us into an oceanic feeling of being at peace with the universe, help us unwind or relax us into deep meditation. It's useful for focus and concentration. It can also rev up our systems to gear up, get off the couch, and party on down!

For those of us on the autism/AS spectrum, music can be useful in so many ways. It's a great tool to help us distinguish complex inner emotions as well as motivating us to accomplish important life tasks.

1. The kind of music I feel like listening to usually corresponds to the type of mood I am in. If I want classical, I'm usually feeling very mellow. Jazz? I feel like being spontaneous. Rock? I feel rebellious. I can even connect classical composers to my various moods. Beethoven? I'm feeling intense. Haydn? Playful. Bach? Intellectual. Rachmaninoff? Brooding and melancholic.

2. Use *musical counterbalancing* to adjust your moods. For example, if I am feeling tense and know I need to relax, I'll put classical on the iPod. If you are feeling angry, listening to heavy metal may not be the best choice. Sometimes, using a musical mood opposite to how you are feeling can actually help change the way you feel. Try it. It works!

3. Before a sporting event, crank up some arena rock or spirited music to get the adrenaline going.

> Before going to sleep, try listening to something more mellow, such as soft rock or classical.

4. I rarely meet individuals with AS who don't like music. Therefore, use your musical interests to connect with others. You'll probably have a lot to contribute. If you can stand the noise, attend live musical events and concerts. It can help you develop an even greater appreciation for the music you love.

Music helps people recharge their batteries in the privacy of their own homes and brings people together in celebration. It can be used in times of mourning or in the celebration of momentous occasions. But for this discussion, most importantly music can act as a therapeutic modality to keep symptoms of depression under control. Whether you listen to music, compose music, play an instrument, or sing, the power of music can act as the high pitched whistle to help keep the black dogs of depression at bay.

And, speaking of dogs…

Having a Pet

I'd like to begin this section by sharing a feature article I wrote for the *Autism Asperger's Digest* (July–August 2010) called "Angel Animals and Autistics: A Love Affair."

> A few weeks ago, an angel came into my life. I don't mean the kind of angel with wings playing a harp in heaven all day long. I mean an angel with four legs and a little tail, who follows me everywhere I go. I mean the kind of angel who picked me to be a lifetime companion. I'm talking about my cockapoo, Sadie.

If you are on the autism spectrum, you've probably noticed that you have an unusually close relationship with animals. Some would even call it a kinship. Famous autistic authors like Liane Holliday Willey, Temple Grandin, Dawn Price Hughes, and Jerry Newport have all expressed a connection with certain animals. Jerry and his wife joined their two families of birds, making eleven birds altogether. Temple's interest has been in cattle, and because of her keen insight into the psychology of cows, pigs, bison, and antelope, she almost single-handedly created a much more humane way of handling these animals before slaughter. McDonald's, Burger King, and Swift among others employ her methods. Temple has written extensively about the nature of animal behavior and postulates that the autistic mind (particularly savants) and the animal mind function in a similar capacity, as was beautifully illustrated in her book, *Animals in Translation*. Liane's heart belongs to *Equus ferus caballus* (horses) while Dawn is a well-known primatologist who felt an early kinship with gorillas. For her, being in the company of gorillas was an escape from the social isolation she experienced as a result of her Asperger syndrome. Can you relate?

My first dog, Samantha, was a beautiful Lhasa Apso-terrier mix. She was the kind of dog a Hollywood studio would have loved to have for the movies. She had beautiful silky fur and a regal way about her. When she walked into a room, it was almost as if she demanded your attention simply due to her majestic beauty. When I walked her, people would constantly stop me and say she was the most beautiful dog they had ever seen. Besides her beauty, she was a very loving dog and my best friend in middle school. I would come home on days when I had been bullied all day and there she'd be, waiting for me. I would wrap my body around her soft fur and she would offer me a consoling and healing energy that helped me make it through the tough years of middle school and high school. Sam could actually read my moods. If she sensed I was sad, she'd immediately jump onto my bed and start licking me. When I went away to college and would come home every weekend, she'd be there waiting for me. It was like she could almost always sense when I was coming home. My parents said she would go to the window around ten minutes before I arrived as if she could anticipate that I was coming home. She was my rock—the one being in the universe that gave me unconditional comfort, love, and support. I was devastated when she died and never thought she could be replaced. But I was mistaken.

I've had two other angels enter my life. After Samantha died, I pushed my parents to get another dog right away but they weren't quite as ready as I was for a new dog. Finally, they got Bailey, a four-year-old rescue dog. Bailey was always my dog. We connected in a way that far surpassed his connection with my parents. As Bailey got to be a senior dog, he became very ill and lost his hearing. Shortly before he died, I adopted my own dog, Sadie, also from a rescue. It was love at first sight. We bonded instantly and she is the perfect dog for me. She is incredibly calm and devoted. She loves to curl up on my lap and gives me all the space I need. I feel so lucky to have found her. At first, I was concerned that having a dog would interfere with my sleep and my comings and goings. But after a day or two with Sadie, those worries vanished. Having Sadie was worth any sacrifice I had to make.

There is no doubt that Sadie has had a positive effect on my moods. She is a powerful antidepressant with four legs and a tail. I take her for at least three walks a day, which guarantees I get regular exercise and a lot of fresh air. And she is always there to greet me when I walk in the door.

My canine friends have taught me how to love, how to look beyond myself, and to take responsibility for the life of another creature. I've learned just as much, if not more, from dogs than from any human I've ever met.

It is rare that I meet someone on the spectrum who doesn't love animals. Truth be told, most autistics and animals get along very well with each other. Why is that? One reason is that they both know how to offer each other unconditional love. Autistics tend to judge others on whether they have earned their respect. Animals are the same way. Autistics and animals are also both extremely sensitive to sensory stimuli. They both communicate in a very direct way. Autistics usually don't beat around the bush when communicating with other people, neither do animals when communicating with their human owners.

If you are considering getting a pet, I would encourage you to follow through with it. Not only do numerous studies indicate that you'll live longer, have a better quality of life, and experience fewer episodes of depression, but you'll spend part of your life with a companion who'll love you for who you are on a daily basis. This can be particularly comforting if you plan on remaining single and living by yourself. Your new best friend will be there throughout and will help see you through the tough times as well as help you celebrate the good times. What more could you ask for in a friend?

In many prisons throughout the country, there are programs in which inmates work to train dogs as aides for those with disabilities or illnesses. There was a study done at the Oakwood Forensic Center in Lima, Ohio, in 1975 where certain inmates were given small pets to care for. As a result of taking care of these animals, the behavior of the inmates radically changed. They needed to take only half as much medication and had fewer incidents of violence and suicide attempts (Dubin 2009). This is hardly a conclusive study but it does demonstrate the potential healing power pets can play in our lives.

Even though the scientific community is currently divided on whether pets actually lower levels of depression, I can see some clear advantages. Pets offer constant companionship. They are completely nonjudgmental of their owner's moods and can often sense when they need cheering up. Many pets are even in tune with their owner's developing low blood sugar levels. Some pets have been reported to sniff out their owner's cancer before it developed into a serious tumor. Others know when a seizure is imminent and try to warn their owners. The remarkable intuitive abilities that certain pets possess can also be invaluable when it comes to lifting their owners' spirits.

Pets are also fun. Whether a cat is chasing its own tail or a dog has rolled over on his back asking to have his belly tickled, they can put a smile on your face in the bleakest of moments.

Additionally, pets force their owners to think about something other than themselves. When you are entrusted with the care of an animal, it's no longer all about you and your suffering. There's a real responsibility involved with taking care of a pet. During those times when you don't feel like getting out of bed, but you have an animal to care for, guess what? You have to get out of bed.

Before deciding to become a pet owner, it is crucial to ask yourself if you're ready to make this commitment. Do you have the financial resources to be able to care for a pet adequately? This would include buying food, getting the necessary equipment (leash, water, food bowls, etc.), and paying for veterinary appointments. Also, make sure the place in which you live, whether it's an apartment or condo, allows you to have pets. And most important, ask yourself if you really love animals enough to make room in your home for one. If so, your new best friend may be an invaluable therapeutic aid in keeping your symptoms of depression under control.

Social Networking Sites

The last ten years have greatly changed the landscape of how people on the spectrum socialize with each other. In addition to in-person meet-up groups, the Internet proliferates with message boards and social networking sites where people with autism and Asperger's like to hang out virtually. Sites like wrongplanet.net, Aspiesforfreedom.com, and Facebook attract thousands of Aspies every day who commiserate and sympathize with each other's pain as well as celebrate the individual and collective successes of the autism community.

Depression can be a very isolating experience. When you are depressed, it can seem as if no one understands the extent of your pain. An obvious advantage of these message boards and social networking sites is that they immediately put you in touch with a group of like-minded people who have experienced similar struggles to your own. Unlike a decade ago when you would have had to look far and wide for an Asperger's meet-up group, you can now locate such groups from the comfort of your own home. The neurodiversity movement was birthed on the Internet. It is unlikely this movement would have started without the use of the Internet, given the fact that the AS population prefers it as a means of communication.

There are also virtual worlds that have become very popular among people with Asperger's. Essentially these virtual worlds allow you to create an avatar to fit whatever appearance you desire and interact in an environment that mirrors real life. Locations that exist in real life also exist in a virtual world, such as bowling alleys, bars, streets, and synagogues. Virtual worlds can be used in the same way as social networking sites: to gain confidence in social skills and to find people who share your struggles and may help you to cope with depression. Some experts even think that virtual worlds can offer vital practice and rehearsal time for social encounters in the real world since they mimic the dynamics of real life. See Phillips (2008) for one such story.

Some experts are skeptical, claiming the strategies learned in virtual worlds do not replicate real life experiences. If you choose to build an online persona using an avatar, it's important that you are able to differentiate between that persona and your real self. If the persona helps you gain confidence, that's great. But if it takes over your identity to the point where you start to devalue your real self, then it is not serving you.

There are some disadvantages and pitfalls to be aware of when it comes to social networking sites. People get their feelings hurt from time to time. Sometimes a person won't accept you as a friend and may send an unfriendly or unflattering message to you. When you are dealing with strangers in a public forum, you are taking a risk. There are always irrational and hostile people out there, and there's no way for them to be screened. Be careful not to let the Internet be the only way you communicate with others. Communicating with people via the Internet is better than not having any outside contact with people, but it can be unhealthy when it is your sole means of relating to others.

Here is a news bite of mine that appeared in the *Autism Asperger's Digest* (November–December 2009) entitled "Social Cyberspace," which further elaborates on this subject.

Second Life, MySpace, Facebook and Twitter: it's hard to believe that virtual friendship and relationship sites did not exist ten years ago. Today users can socialize, meet new people, and reconnect with old chums without having to leave the house. Maybe this is good; maybe it's not so good. For the person with Asperger's, social networking sites have their pros and cons.

Pros

1. They can serve as dress rehearsals for actual face-to-face encounters. They allow you to practice skills necessary for successful socialization but in a much more relaxed setting.

2. They provide a wider opportunity to meet new people with similar interests and in a less threatening social setting.

3. You can meet other individuals with AS on websites like www.wrongplanet.net and www.Aspiesforfreedom.com for friendship, advice, and a sense of community and solidarity with other like-minded individuals.

Cons

1. If you're not careful, social networking sites have the potential to become addictive and can easily

replace face-to-face encounters. Consciously limit the time you use these websites every day to an hour or two. Use them to gain confidence in your social skills. Don't use them to shield yourself from meeting people, unless you want to feed into the addiction even more.

2. Not everyone who is a friend of yours on Facebook or Twitter is an actual, real-life friend. Many people are friends by association, such as the cousin of your best friend. Rejection happens all the time to people on these websites. Try not to take it too personally.

3. Also, be careful not to divulge too much personal information. If you have 300 friends on Facebook, ask yourself if you want all of them to know every single private detail of your life. Beyond your friends, you are potentially sharing information with the entire world since once something is posted, it has the potential to go viral. Just because others are sharing a lot about themselves doesn't mean you have to. On the other hand, if you are an overly private person, sharing some information about yourself may be a good way to stretch yourself socially. Always keep in mind that employers and potential employers are now looking at your posts and profiles on these sites. Don't share anything that might cast you in a negative light in getting or keeping a job.

Choosing a Therapist

Having a therapist to confide in when you are depressed can be essential. I'm not referring to someone you might reach in an emergency if you called a suicide hotline. I am talking about someone with whom you have a trusting relationship and who understands you inside and out. This person would be someone to whom you can tell things that you wouldn't tell anyone else, including your parents or your best friend. Someone who can bring you back to reality when you start to catastrophize, beat yourself up, or hold yourself up to impossible standards. A competent therapist will not sugarcoat what he or she has to say. If he or she is doing the job correctly, the therapist will tell you what you *need* to hear, not what you *want* to hear.

The dilemma facing many adults on the spectrum is finding a good therapist, since very few specialize in the adult AS population. One question I am often asked is whether a psychotherapist needs to specialize in Asperger syndrome in order to be effective. It would be ideal to find a therapist who specializes in working with adults on the spectrum. However, that qualification is not always possible to find in a therapist, especially in rural areas where there aren't a lot of qualified professionals to choose from. If the therapist doesn't specialize in Asperger's, it is important that he or she expresses a willingness to learn about it. Ask the therapist if he or she would attend a seminar or at least read some books on the subject. If you get a negative response, look for someone else.

In choosing a therapist, credentials matter. Make sure this person has a doctoral or master's degree in psychology, neuropsychology, social work, or counseling from an accredited institution. Most psychiatrists these days primarily prescribe medications and can refer you to someone else for psychological counseling.

The most important qualification for a therapist is that you feel comfortable relating to that person. You will know almost immediately whether this is the case. If you have any discomfort around this person, trust your instincts. It is also a good idea to shop around. Do not select someone out of expedience or because you read a good review on the Internet. Take the time to ask people in your community for referrals. If you do not feel comfortable doing this yourself, perhaps one of your parents, a sibling, or friend would help you with this process.

Getting Adequate Sleep

Insomnia is a common problem for Aspies. Part of the reason is due to sensory differences. Because autistics are hypersensitive, being awake at night when it is dark is sometimes easier than during the day when it is light and sunny. I also believe there's a rumination component going on as well. Many people with Asperger's have told me they stay up late and replay the day's events in their heads, analyzing everything to death and thinking about what they could have done differently.

Lack of sleep can exacerbate one's depression. When circadian rhythms are thrown off, the body doesn't know when to secrete hormones and one's alertness is affected. Unfortunately what sets the circadian rhythm clock into motion is exposure to sunlight. Many people with Asperger's are sensory defensive and prefer to be away from the sun and live with the drapes closed. Stephen Shore notes that he hasn't met a single individual with autism who doesn't have sensory integration issues. He cites one man who claimed he didn't have any sensory issues but always pulled down the shades and turned off the lights in his home to live in the dark (Shore 2006).

I believe another reason those with Asperger's have trouble sleeping is because of a pronounced fear of death. A poll taken on www.wrongplanet.net asked Aspies how often they think about death and dying in a week. Forty percent said they thought about it more than ten times a week (wrongplanet.net 2008). This statistic means that Aspies are thinking about death at least once a day, possibly more. This is an unconscious fear that can exacerbate insomnia because thinking about death may create concerns of losing consciousness.

Freud remarked that dreaming is the royal road to the unconscious. When you fall asleep, your unconscious has free rein over your conscious mind. Thoughts, emotions, hidden motives, and even shadow qualities show up in dreams. Dream content can be scary, especially for a person who likes to have precise control over his or her thoughts. In a dreaming state, such control doesn't exist. It is therefore threatening to fall asleep, since dreaming can represent a loss of control. For some, conscious rumination and unpleasant thoughts can be more appealing than dreams.

Not being on a consistent sleep schedule will make depression worse, so it is important to do everything possible to stay on track. Here are a few suggestions:

- Your bedroom should only be used for sleeping or relaxing activities. If your computer is located in your bedroom, you run the risk of being over-stimulated by e-mails, Facebook communications, and work projects, and your bedroom will quickly become associated with stress.

- If a particular activity is over-stimulating, make sure you stop doing it at least an hour or two before bedtime. Sometimes watching television before bedtime can be relaxing, but it all depends on the show. The same goes for reading. If a particular book gets you overanalyzing its content to the point where your mind can't slow down, perhaps it's not a good idea to read it right before bed.

- Consider buying a sound machine to use while you are trying to fall asleep. I sometimes use several in addition to a noisy fan and they drown out all other noises. A sound machine can simulate the sound of rain, waves coming up on shore, birds chirping, or a babbling brook. I'm an extremely hypersensitive sleeper and can hear almost everything around me. With the sound machine on, I can even sleep through a severe thunderstorm. The sounds also tend to block any disturbing thoughts I might be having. If you use one of these machines, you might need to buy an extra-loud alarm clock that can penetrate through the noise made by the sound machine.

- Once in bed, try to let go of all unpleasant thoughts. When such a thought comes into consciousness, simply say to yourself, "That's interesting," almost flippantly. Attach no emotional significance to the thought and let it go. Don't start getting analytical as your head is touching the pillow. The mantra when falling asleep should be "Silence is golden."

• Think about taking a natural sleep aid, but only under the proper supervision of a doctor. Be aware of any side effects the sleep aid might have. On rare occasions I have taken melatonin or valerian, and they have helped me on nights when I have been unable to fall asleep. However, I notice I'm usually a little drowsier the next day.

When you wake up in the morning, give yourself some time to transition from the world of sleep and dreams into reality. Many people don't realize that this transition from unconsciousness to wakefulness can be difficult due to the processing of dream content. If you know that waking up requires some transition time, make sure you plan for that as you schedule your day.

Exercise

A proper diet and a sufficient amount of daily exercise are essential in dealing with symptoms of depression. Since those with Asperger's tend to be ritual-minded, I suggest making exercise a regular part of your daily routine. Incrementally increase the amount of activity you do each day until you reach a healthy baseline. This is a prerequisite to avoid becoming diabetic, developing early Alzheimer's, having heart disease, and speeding the aging process. Exercise produces the body's own morphine—endorphins—which can act as painkillers and produce feelings of pleasure (hence the term "runner's high"). If you live in an area where outdoor exercise is not possible in the winter, consider investing in a stationary exercise bike or a treadmill. If you have the resources, you might think about joining a gym. Many workout facilities offer fairly reasonable memberships for less than $25 a month. High-end places will likely have more amenities.

Gratitude

The practice of gratitude is always the perfect antidote for depression, even if you are just grateful for being alive. If you can appreciate the present moments in your life, you will find those moments add up. Appreciate what you have, whether it's a pet that loves you, an outstanding music collection, or a friend you can depend on. Train your mind to be grateful for what you have rather than what you don't have in life. Practice showing gratitude to the universe (with or without God) when something good happens to you. Allow yourself to enjoy what you might not even notice, like the smell of the tulips blooming in spring, the sound of rain on your windowpane, or someone holding a door open for you when you walk into a store. There are some beautiful moments in life that can easily be missed when we're embroiled in our own mental misery.

My grandfather was 89 years old when he died. He expressed his gratitude about the little things in life on a daily basis. I visited him in a nursing home a few days before he died. As I was leaving to say goodbye for what looked likely to be the last time, I asked him how he was doing. He responded with a smile, "No complaints." His attitude of being grateful served him well, right up until the end of his life.

Dating

One of the biggest sources of depression among adults with Asperger's is undoubtedly the lack of success in the dating arena. Here are some points to keep in mind when entering the world of dating.

Aspies are notorious for being late bloomers. When they finally enter the dating scene in their 20s and 30s, they often feel like kindergarteners who have to study calculus. Compared to neurotypicals who have years of experience under their belts, they are at a distinct disadvantage. The prospect of competing against others with more experience and skill is justifiably terrifying. But there's another rational way to look at it. No one expects you to find a girlfriend or boyfriend as fast as a neurotypical. Just as you may have been given extended time when taking tests in school, give yourself some extended time to get your feet wet in dating. Also, you may have to experience more than your fair share of rejection before you find the right person. Personalizing this rejection is something you'll have to work hard at to avoid. Instead, channel the famous Aspie determination (some might call it perseveration) and focus on finding the right person. However, if someone is not interested in pursuing a relationship with you, you must respect his or her wishes.

Take stock in what you have to offer someone in a relationship. Are you faithful? Do you communicate directly? Do you like to spend time alone as well as time with your partner? Do you judge people more on their personal qualities than their physical appearance? If you answered "yes" to those questions, there is probably someone out there who would want to meet you. While we live in a culture that tends to value people who are gregarious, outgoing, funny, and socially adept, all it takes is one special person to love and appreciate you for whom you are. It might just take a little longer to find him or her.

Employment

Sadly, the AS population is largely unemployed and underemployed. Not only does this unfortunate situation affect socioeconomic status, it also has an impact on the ability to obtain health insurance, to leave the family nest, and to be self-sufficient. Moreover, being unemployed or underemployed can also cause severe depression. The biggest problem is that most employment settings are not friendly toward individuals on the spectrum and require social skills that are a challenge for people with Asperger's.

Corporate culture is apparent everywhere. From employee uniforms and codes of conduct to customer service scripts and clueless human resource managers, Aspies have to fight an uphill battle to gain access to worthwhile jobs. Disposability of employees is more rampant than ever. Assuming you are lucky enough to get your foot in the door for an interview, you are still at an incredible disadvantage when competing against people more socially skilled than you are.

I had a conversation with a therapist who runs a thriving counseling practice, treating adults on the spectrum as well as parents of children and teenagers on the spectrum. I expressed my frustration that so many Aspies I knew were either not being hired or in job settings that were well below their qualifications. The therapist believes that one option for people on the spectrum is micro enterprising. This is a type of small business consisting of four or five employees and does not require much capital. One concern I had about this type of venture was the ability of someone with Asperger's to run a business due to organizational and executive functioning challenges. His response was that an Aspie could bring in others who have strengths in those areas. That made perfect sense. Ideally, each person's skills would complement those of the group.

As a person with Asperger's, do you have a skill that is marketable? Maybe you are a whiz at putting tractor lawn mowers together. Perhaps you are talented at drawing and can create illustrations. Maybe you excel at software development. Are you always fixing other people's computers? Perhaps you could turn these abilities into a business. If you have a particular skill, the idea would be to pair yourself with others who have a similar vision.

If the idea of micro enterprising doesn't appeal to you or you don't think you have a viable skill, consider working in a non-corporate environment. The best kind of job might be in a small setting where communication doesn't have to be filtered through bureaucratic structures. If you have expertise or knowledge in a given subject, teaching might be a good career track. Many Aspies have found their place in academia.

If you aren't college-educated, consider working in a smaller type of environment without an overwhelming number of employees or sensory distractions. If you are a music whiz or have some special interest, a store dealing in your subject matter would be the perfect fit. It's true you would have to interact with customers, but it would be on your terms and in an area about which you are knowledgeable.

Being gainfully employed would certainly help alleviate symptoms of depression. Although people with Asperger's may have to work a lot harder to find the right employment fit, the rewards couldn't be sweeter. In addition to the pay, employment will provide a sense of satisfaction and accomplishment as your skills and talents are being put to good use and you're making a positive impact on the world.

Self-disclosure

Choosing the people to whom you disclose your Asperger's diagnosis can also have an impact on depression. If most people in your life are aware of your diagnosis, you will probably have fewer communication misunderstandings. At work, it will make it easier to be yourself and help you to breathe a giant sigh of relief. Just as some gay people are proud to disclose who they are openly, people with Asperger's can take pride in being able to state who they are openly, without feelings of shame. I've seen many individuals on the spectrum take pride in having Asperger's, which has contributed immeasurably to their self-esteem. However, disclosure isn't always appropriate or even realistic. The following is an article I wrote for the *Autism Asperger's Digest* (May–June 2010) entitled "The Art of Self-Disclosure."

> One question I often get asked at speaking engagements pertains to self-disclosure. Frequently this question comes in the form of a parent asking me when I think their child is old enough to handle the news of his or her own diagnosis. But just as frequently an adult on the spectrum will ask me whether self-disclosure is warranted or justified. Each case and circumstance is different but there are some general guidelines to keep in mind.
>
> Obviously, there's no need to disclose to most strangers or people with whom you have only brief interactions, such as the checkout person at the supermarket, the clerk at the dry cleaners, or your mailman. What about family members?

I would say it depends on the person. My grandmother, who is in her 90s, knows about my Asperger's but has a hard time grasping the concept simply because of her age and the generational gap that exists between us. Many of my uncles, aunts, and cousins have appreciated knowing about my AS because it explained befuddling traits such as aloofness, idiosyncratic behaviors, and my special interests. Yet my parents were initially resistant to the idea that I might have a developmental disability because they feared it would result in many broken dreams for me. In time, they have come to accept and even embrace the diagnosis. Unfortunately many of my fellow Aspies have not been so lucky, never gaining parental or familial support after they disclosed to their families.

It is important to realize self-disclosure is not a one-time conversation, and most often you will be educating people who know far less than you do about autism or Asperger's. Most of the general public is uninformed or misinformed when it comes to AS, especially if it has never touched their lives in a personal way. When you tell your Uncle Harry you have Asperger's, he may not appreciate what that means. You'll want to explain to your uncle what Asperger syndrome is, the positive attributes you have as a result of having it, as well as some of the challenges it brings. Uncle Harry may still be a little confused or have some additional questions for you. If so, reassure him this is a very natural reaction and you'd be happy to answer any further questions. Try not to feel bad if people seem a bit dazed and confused when you self-disclose to them. This will happen from time to time, but it is more a reflection of their lack of understanding and the embarrassment this causes them than a judgment being imposed on you.

Perhaps the biggest question that arises for individuals with Asperger's is whether or not to initially disclose to potential romantic interests or future employers. Imagine going on a first date with someone who tells you they have dyslexia. Some people might be a little uncomfortable hearing this simply because it's such a personal statement to make to someone you don't know very well. It's not that dyslexia is a bad thing or something to be judged but conversation topics tend to be more superficial at the beginning of most relationships. "What's your sign? What do you do for a living? What do you do for fun?" These kinds of surface topics don't come easily to many people with Asperger's since they tend to like meatier, more substantive matters to discuss. However, my advice would be to let the other person get to know you and appreciate you for who you are before disclosing your Asperger's. Eventually it will be something that will need to be disclosed to avoid communicational misunderstandings that can happen to an Aspie-neurotypical couple.

What about future employers? The same principle applies. It is not wise to tell a potential boss about something he or she might perceive as a liability even if you are presenting it as a strength or an asset. In our bottom-line, free-market, capitalist-driven economy, employers usually care about one thing—productivity. Though they legally cannot discriminate against you having Asperger's, most people know there are always ways around this. Therefore try and get your foot in the door before disclosing. Once you have done this, you can let your boss know areas of the job in which you will be likely to excel and areas in which you may have more difficulty. This can be done without ever disclosing the Asperger's, and it can also be done through the help of a job coach. However you choose to disclose your diagnosis, let your boss know about your potential limitations before the first incident arises. Bosses typically don't like being told about a disability after a mistake because they often perceive it as using the Asperger's as an excuse.

Telling other people you have Asperger's is a bit like coming out of the closet. It can be freeing after a lifetime of confusion. Yet you still need to be careful as to when, how, and to whom you disclose. And you need to be sufficiently self-aware and hold a positive attitude toward yourself and AS to self-disclose in a way that doesn't make you sound pitiful. Remember: the opinion you hold of yourself during self-disclosure is usually the opinion others will form about you. Once you get skilled in the art of self-disclosure, you'll intuitively know when it's appropriate and the most effective ways to do it.

Self-consciousness

If you tend to be self-conscious, my message to you is live through your eyes, not your head. The information your eyes reflect back to you is completely impartial. Only the mind can make you become so conscious of your every move that you begin to pay more attention to what's going on inside your head than what's happening right in front of your eyes. There is no surer way to become depressed than to be overly self-conscious. Living in your head is what your inner critic thrives on.

When I am self-conscious, I only pay attention to critical thoughts about myself. My attention is squarely focused inward not outward. By living through your eyes and not your head, you turn off that voice that interjects negative comments about every move you make. When I played competitive tennis, I had to lose all self-consciousness and totally merge myself with the activity to play. Whenever I thought about what my coach or others might be thinking about my game or the repercussions of losing, I would make an error. When I wasn't self-conscious it didn't mean I won every point, but it greatly improved the chances that I would be more successful.

If you have to be self-conscious, it should be when you are alone and not with other people. Try to be self-conscious in a productive way. Gently remind yourself that any social faux pas or banana-peel slips you might have made are just par for the course. Instead of berating yourself for these mistakes, learn from them. Even try to laugh at yourself. A little self-deprecation never hurt anyone, as long as it's done lightheartedly.

The Greatness of Asperger's

I want to close this chapter with an article that appeared in the *Autism Asperger's Digest* (2009) entitled "The Greatness of Asperger's." I hope that reading this article will lift your spirits when you are feeling down.

The great Henry David Thoreau once said that men are born to succeed, not fail. Yet, looking around at our medically based culture, which in general focuses on deficits and pathology rather than strengths and well-being, you would never know it. Just read the *Diagnostic and Statistical Manual of Mental Disorders (DSM)*, and skim the hundreds of pages of diseases and disorders plaguing mankind. It's a wonder anybody is considered normal these days. There seems to be a disorder associated with just about anything.

Shortly after I received my diagnosis of Asperger syndrome in 2004, I became frustrated and depressed, not because of the diagnosis per se, but because of how it was characterized. Everything I read described only the deficits and limitations associated with it. Could this be all that was written? It became my personal quest to scour the literature for a book, an article, anything that would be the antithesis to the doom and gloom perspective of the *DSM*. Was there anything written that might correlate positive qualities or character virtues to specific Asperger's traits?

Lucky for me, the first piece of literature I came across was Tony Attwood and Carol Gray's article, "The Discovery of 'Aspie' Criteria." The title certainly looked intriguing, and the content did not disappoint. To my utter delight, the words on the pages tickled my senses and had me jumping for joy. Gray and Attwood had written what was essentially a mock *DSM* entry for Asperger syndrome, focused on the positive attributes people with AS display. Among the qualities listed was the observation that people with AS tend to be free of culturist, ageist, or sexist judgments, instead regarding others at face value. This rang true for me. Another attribute was that people with AS tend to speak their minds, irrespective of social context or adherence to personal beliefs. Check, also me. In fact, they listed 28 positive characteristics, and the vast majority resonated with me, based on both my own experience and my relationships with fellow Aspies.

I started discovering other relevant literature and, surprisingly, some of it had absolutely nothing to do with AS, but nonetheless offered its own close connections. One particular author captured my attention, Mihaly Csikszentmihalyi, a Hungarian psychologist who wrote the groundbreaking 1990 book entitled *Flow: The Psychology of Optimal Experience*. Csikszentmihalyi is known in psychology circles as a positive psychologist, noted for his work in the areas of happiness and creativity. As a researcher, he tries to understand what qualities need to be in place for an individual to thrive in his or her environment. In writing *Flow*, he described a state similar to what athletes call being in the zone, where time and sense of self fade away and it feels like you can do no wrong. Flow happens when you are fully engaged and immersed in whatever it is you are doing. Most of us experience that flow state from time to time in our lives, often when we are involved in something that is highly interesting to us.

Csikszentmihalyi identified certain personal qualities that are paramount to achieving the flow state. With my insider knowledge of AS, I realized that Aspies have an inherent advantage in reaching this state over our neurotypical counterparts. Every quality Csikszentmihalyi lists requires an intense and unwavering amount of focus and concentration, qualities many Aspies have in spades. I cannot count the number of times I have observed people with AS so fully engaged in an activity that they are completely oblivious to everyone and everything around them. It is almost as if the person and the activity merge into one. Normally, this behavior would be viewed as negative, or perhaps referred to as self-absorption or stimming (jargon for stereotypy). But filtering these behaviors through Csikszentmihalyi's eyes, we can appreciate that they serve a positive function. Csikszentmihalyi also feels that the flow state is reached only when the activity is intrinsically rewarding. Can you imagine an Aspie thriving at something that wasn't intrinsically rewarding? I rest my case. When people with AS find an activity they can take pleasure in, most of them are incredibly innovative, creative, and express their talent effortlessly. Csikszentmihalyi described other qualities that characterize the flow state:

1. *Clear goals.* A laser-sharp understanding of what needs to be accomplished.

2. A sense of personal *control* over the situation or activity.

3. *A distorted sense of time.* Working at the computer and thinking fifteen minutes has gone by when it's actually been two hours.

4. *Focus and concentration.* A high degree of concentration on a focused field of attention.

People familiar with the characteristics of AS will undoubtedly recognize that they overlap those of Csikszentmihalyi's to a large degree. Small wonder so many geniuses are suspected of having AS. However, you don't have to be a savant or have a super high IQ score to be good at tapping into flow. You just have to be passionate about whatever it is you're doing.

As my search continued, I discovered a few more authors who were enlightened enough to recognize other positive AS qualities. These authors did so through studying famous people. Michael Fitzgerald (*Genius Genes: How Asperger Talents Changed the World*) and Norm Ledgin (*Asperger's and Self-Esteem: Insight and Hope Through Famous Role Models* and *Diagnosing Jefferson*) both believe that some remarkable individuals throughout the course of history have been Aspies. Perhaps the most well-known is Albert

Einstein, but others come to mind—Thomas Jefferson, Isaac Newton, Glenn Gould, Ludwig Wittgenstein, Immanuel Kant, Tim Page, and Daniel Tammet. Every one of these individuals clearly demonstrated an ability to tap into the flow state almost at will. I can picture Glenn Gould, world famous pianist, with an otherworldly look on his face playing the music of Bach or Daniel Tammet, as he learned Icelandic in less than a week and recited Pi to the 20,000th digit.

During my research, I was the most excited finding the work of renowned positive psychologists Martin Seligman and Christopher Peterson. These two scholars wanted to create a classification system that would be the counterpart to the *DSM*. Using their 20-plus years of research, they did so, and described it in their book, ***Character Strengths and Virtues***. Seligman and Peterson isolate different character strengths and analyze the causes, correlates, and consequences of each.

Maybe I'm a bit biased, but as I read through their list of causes and correlates, I couldn't help but see the AS population mirrored in their descriptions. Take creativity, for example. Seligman and Peterson view creativity as a prerequisite for wisdom. Many Aspies tend to be creative as well as displaying originality and ingenuity. Creativity can develop as a coping mechanism when a person has difficulty assimilating to one's surroundings. Having AS, that's often our experience. Our lives can feel like visiting a different foreign country every day, with its unfamiliar language, customs, rules, and rituals. One has to be savvy and learn to think outside the box to survive. Growing up within a culture that many of us cannot comprehend or even accept, we often come up with new ideas, different ways of looking at old problems, and sustainable solutions for a changing world. Because we often cannot function like a cog in a well-oiled machine, instead, we like to build the machine ourselves.

This is when our creativity truly flourishes and our inner wisdom unfolds. Open-mindedness is another positive quality on Seligman and Peterson's list. It is true that we Aspies may be close-minded about our daily routines and rituals, preferring not to deviate from what is familiar, but anecdotal evidence suggests that we are not close-minded regarding how we view the world. Many AS individuals I have met hold fundamental beliefs that differ from those held by their parents. The vast majority of them see things differently from the mainstream on issues such as religion, politics, social issues, and spirituality. Perhaps being born in a neurological minority correlates with understanding life on one's own terms, not society's terms. This ability to look within oneself and draw important truths about the world is open-mindedness in its highest form, a quality highly valued among the Buddhists and spiritual practitioners.

Peterson and Seligman list other positive character strengths, such as persistence and vitality, which correlate to being courageous. They talk about kindness in terms of being selflessly altruistic, caring, and generous. They speak of justice, connecting to both fairness and leadership. These qualities are part and parcel of individuals with AS, and if you know such individuals or are an Aspie yourself, you already know this is true. We hold these truths to be self-evident!

I attained my goal to find positive expressions about what it means to have AS. It was not accomplished without months of research. Many of my fellow Aspies don't have the luxury of conducting such an investigation. Society has yet to catch up and view our differences in a positive light, yet the inklings of change exist. Individuals with Asperger's have endured and flourished through the generations. This would not occur if we had nothing valuable to offer.

On days when those of us with AS find ourselves feeling depressed or anxious because the world looks at us with blinders on, remember that we are a unique and special group who bring many gifts and insights to the world at large. Here are some other thoughts to keep in mind to help stay positive:

- Embrace your gifts. Recognize your common humanity and brotherhood with others while celebrating your individuality and creativity.

- Dare to dream! If you can dream it, you can achieve it.

- Follow your passions and success will follow.

- Don't lose hope. Our life's purpose is often hidden to us. Maybe you are here to help others expand their perspectives and discover new possibilities.

- Be a leader. Help other Aspies recognize their potential and realize their dreams. Help society at large recognize us as positive, contributing members of our communities. As Gandhi once said, "Be the change you want to see in the world."

Chapter 9

Interview with My Parents

In my last two books, *Asperger Syndrome and Bullying* (2007) and *Asperger Syndrome and Anxiety* (2009), I interviewed my parents regarding these subjects. I received positive feedback about the information my parents provided, so I am doing it again with the topic of depression. I know many of you reading this book are parents of children on the autism spectrum. I hope that something my parents say will resonate with or be helpful to you.

I want to preface their remarks by giving a general description of my relationship with them.

I have been very fortunate to have parents who have shown me love and support throughout my life. Sometimes I feel guilty that not all Aspies have been so fortunate. No one gets to choose their parents, as is true with all aspects of life. We have to make the best of the cards we are dealt.

My mother is a bright and creative person. She is a playwright and also teaches playwriting at a state university. She is a fairly emotional person and that personality trait serves her well in her work. She genuinely loves teaching her students as well as seeing her work produced. She also has a wonderful sense of humor.

During my teen years, we often didn't get along because my emotional makeup clashed with hers. We both tended to be reactive to each other. Part of the problem was that I had not been diagnosed with Asperger's when I was a teenager. Therefore, my parents concluded that my lack of socializing was more of a psychological problem than a neurological one. My mom would constantly pressure me to call friends, go to dances, or find some group to join. The more she pushed, the more I pushed back. It got pretty hairy at times. Receiving my diagnosis really helped clarify things and provided a major shift in our relationship. Instead of seeing me as being oppositional, she understood where I was coming from. Also, the more mature I have become, the more I am able to see my contribution to our difficult times together. She has also come to recognize her contribution to our past conflicts. We are both calmer now and less quick to anger. I see my mother as someone who loves me, supports me, and really wants nothing but the best things in life for me.

My dad is very different than my mother. He is a lawyer who did trial work for many years and then became a respected law professor who teaches legal ethics. He is more rational and less emotional than my mother or me, but he is more defensive in nature when it comes to receiving criticism. While I was growing up, he was extremely supportive of me. We went on many father–son trips, and he encouraged me to play competitive tennis.

I still need to work on my relationship with my parents, to become more independent from them, and view them as separate from myself. I admire them as individuals, and they respect the progress I have made in becoming my own person.

It is interesting that both of my parents put themselves out in the world. My mom does so with her plays and my dad expresses himself publicly on legal matters on radio, television, and in the print media. I have emulated this quality, and it has helped me in terms of my writing and public speaking.

I interviewed each of my parents separately and asked them the same questions. They did not hear each other's answers.

Nick: How old was I when you first noticed I was depressed? How did I behave?

Mom: I observed you being sad at times during elementary school but what I would now term depression began in earnest in middle school. You would always come home in a bad mood and pick fights, mostly with me, and be very ornery. It was very frustrating. At the time, I thought you were just being oppositional. It took me a long time to connect your anger and combativeness with depression.

Dad: There seems to be different ways to answer this question according to how I would define depression. If depression means showing outward signs of distress and despondency, then I noticed these signs while you were in high school. However, if depression means something less severe, perhaps I noticed signs starting as early as nursery school. When you were that age, you had a core sense of energy and happiness that I always enjoyed. Looking at pictures of you at a young age, you don't see a depressed child at all.

When you started preschool at the age of three or four, you were not fitting in with the rest of the kids. Your teachers would say that you wouldn't socialize. I think you knew you were not fitting in and were upset by that fact. You were too young to articulate your feelings but old enough to feel them. The discomfort you experienced and the recognition that you were different from other children made you feel bad about yourself. Although I didn't think of you being depressed then, that's probably what was going on.

When you started kindergarten, your sadness about school was a puzzle to me. I didn't know if it was related to your delayed speech, which had been substantially remedied by that time through speech therapy. Some of your teachers told us you had gifted qualities despite your learning or behavior issues. There were major gaps between your performance level at school and your inherent intelligence. That gap persisted throughout your public school education. You were never diagnosed with Asperger's during your school years (1983–1996) because that diagnosis wasn't officially recognized until 1994.

Nick: How did my symptoms of depression change as I grew older?

Mom: When you started middle school, all hell broke loose. You would come home from school extremely sad, frustrated, and angry. And it wasn't like we could talk about it with you either. You just blew into the house like a white tornado, and I would sometimes have to cower in the corner and wait until you were able to calm down.

That was the period of time when you were being bullied a lot. These episodes had a devastating effect on you. You would have meltdowns and be filled with rage. Did I recognize that as depression? Unfortunately, not right away. The bullying situation was difficult. At the time there were no policies in place at your middle school for dealing with bullying. Dad and I were frustrated that the problem was not being taken seriously enough. Like most parents in that situation, we felt helpless.

In high school you were able to articulate your feelings more, so that made things a little easier. We could all sit down as a family and you could vent to us about what was bothering you. But it would take quite a while for you to calm yourself down and to get in touch with what was upsetting you before you could actually verbalize it.

Dad: When you were in elementary school, you seemed to internalize your differences with other children on many levels. You didn't want to participate in any group social activities. You preferred to engage in parallel play. You lacked the fine motor skills other children had, and I'm sure you were aware of your inability to perform the kinds of skills teachers in nursery and grade school asked of you, for example cutting and pasting and coloring within the lines. So you would wander around the classroom by yourself while other students were doing what they were supposed to, and some teachers thought you were intentionally not willing to do what was required. When you would come home from school, you were happy to be out of that environment and enjoyed not stressing out over the demands placed on you at school.

You went to a private nursery school where you were given some latitude to be yourself and move at your own pace. When you started kindergarten at public school, you faced a much more regimented structure in which you had to stay in your seat most of the day, walk in a straight line in the hallways, and not talk to other children during class. At first, this new environment made you very uncomfortable because you were having trouble controlling your desire to move around when you wanted to. In first grade, you were very unhappy but as the years of elementary school went on, you adapted fairly well. As long as your teacher understood that you had some special needs, you actually started to like school. In fact by the end of the fifth grade, you received the award for the most improved student in your entire elementary school.

You also made some significant gains in the social arena. After school, you enjoyed having a friend come over or going over to a friend's house to play. You did pretty well socially on a one-to-one basis. In fact, you had two friends that you got together with quite often. These two boys came over to our house a lot, we even took them on a trip with us. It was reassuring that you had these two friendships. One afternoon, I was home and heard you screaming outside the house. I looked in the park behind our house and saw you and these two friends. They had handcuffed you to the monkey bars. I couldn't believe what I was seeing. I tore out of the house and came over to where you were. I was furious at these boys who were clearly taking advantage of you, and I read them the riot act. This episode turned out to be the end of your friendship with them. This disturbed you a great deal because there were no other friends waiting to replace them.

Socializing in groups posed more problems. Going to birthday parties was difficult for you, especially if the theme of the party involved a skill that you were deficient in. For example, a party where you had to ice skate or do some sort of art project created great stress. You didn't want to be with peers when you had to engage in activities that exposed your weaknesses. Mom and I would frequently hold our breath to see how you were feeling when you would come home from this type of event.

Middle school was the beginning of a new era and probably the start of more overt and intense signs of depression. The middle school you attended was hell-bent on preparing students for high school, where you would then be expected to apply to a top-ranked college. Each student was like a mound of cookie dough ready to be formed in the same shaped cookie as every other student. General education teachers did not seem to be knowledgeable or willing to deal with special needs. Also, starting in the sixth grade, you had a locker for the first time. With so many different classes to attend and different papers to keep track of, your locker was a perpetual mess. In addition, you had a great deal of homework that you had no interest in doing and your organizational skills were sorely lacking. Other kids were becoming more social, which involved teasing and bullying. By the end of the day, you would come home having controlled your emotions at school and then you would blow off steam at Mom and me. I'm sure your tirades were due to all types of frustration, from having to go back to school every day for something you forgot to being the victim of anti-Semitic remarks.

In high school, you distinguished yourself as a tennis star by playing number one singles for four years, taking your team to the state finals, and being named the most valuable player on your team. Despite all those achievements, the signs of depression were becoming much more visible. You didn't want to be around school one second more than you had to. You would come home for lunch every day to unwind. Other than tennis, you didn't socialize with others and seemed very unhappy. Although you had so much success in tennis and were frequently featured in the sports section of the local paper, you were almost completely isolated from your peers. I'm sure the seeds of depression that began at an earlier age were now starting to germinate. The signs of full-blown depression became visible when you went away to college.

At the time, you thought peers would judge you negatively if you didn't go away to college because that's what everyone else was doing. In reality you were very frightened about leaving home and not having our support in what would be a socially challenging environment. After visiting a number of colleges in Michigan and Indiana, you decided to attend Grand Valley State University near Grand Rapids. You would be playing number one singles on their varsity tennis team, and it seemed the best fit in terms of academic support.

From the day we dropped you off at college, your life became a nightmare. What we had previously seen as unhappiness was now symptomatic of severe anxiety and depression. Dorm life was unbearable for you. There was too much noise, no social support, and the absence of having your own space. After a few weeks, you were in such a crisis that we had to move you out of the dorm and into a private rooming house where you had a room to yourself in the basement. The woman who rented to you was a devout Christian and spent a great deal of time trying to convert you from Judaism to accepting Christianity as your faith. One weekend when you came home, I remember a bible fell out of your suitcase that she had put in it. I had to make a special trip to her home to ask her to stop the religious harassment.

College life was extremely difficult for you. Some weekends, you and I would meet halfway in Lansing and go to a movie or talk about the problems of adjusting to college life. My goal was to help you get your head on straight for the upcoming week. Many weekends, you would drive home through a snowstorm just to get away from school. I never thought you would finish that year, but to my amazement you did. As a result of your inner strength, you were able to play great tennis and get decent grades, all while under great stress and pressure.

You decided not to return to Grand Valley after your freshman year and the following fall transferred to Oakland University, which was a short commute from our home. Although you had to give up tennis because Oakland didn't have a team, moving back home was a security blanket for you. Now you could go to class, have your own radio show on the campus station, and not have as much of the stress as you had experienced during your first year away at college. After receiving your BA in communications from Oakland University, you decided to enroll in a double master's program at the University of Detroit Mercy, majoring in education and learning disabilities. You did extremely well in your class work, but when the time came to student teach in a second grade classroom, things fell apart. When you and your supervisor teacher decided that teaching elementary school wasn't a good fit for you, a full-blown depression ensued.

Without being a therapist, I recognized that you were in a severe depression. You didn't want to leave your apartment and refused to engage in activities that you normally loved to do (e.g. playing tennis, going to concerts). You expressed a sense of hopelessness about the future. You brought up feelings of suicide. This depression didn't come out of the blue, but rather was the inevitable product of a long history of negative feelings and experiences.

Shortly thereafter, you were diagnosed with Asperger's when you were 27 years old. Since then, your depression has greatly lifted in terms of severity. Despite the challenges you still face, you have obtained your doctorate in psychology, written highly regarded books, produced documentaries, and become a sought-after public speaker. These accomplishments took place since your diagnosis and have helped you find your self-worth. I am impressed by your strength and your ability to turn your life around.

Nick: How have you felt about my struggles with my sexuality?

Mom: That is a very painful question to answer. I have watched you go through many years of turmoil and anguish about this issue and felt powerless to help you come to terms with it. From adolescence on, you suffered with so much confusion and because you were never involved in any romantic relationships, you were not entirely sure of your sexuality. Recently, you have finally come to accept your sexual orientation and have disclosed this information publicly for the first time in this book. I couldn't be more proud of you.

Dad: That's perhaps the most interesting question you have posed. Sex seems like such a bombshell of a topic and I have great respect for your willingness to be so honest about the struggles you have endured. I know how difficult it was for you to socialize with peers during the formative years of your sexual development and I remember the bullying you experienced around that issue and the torment it caused.

My most vivid memory is of the pain you had when you first tried to tell me you thought you might be gay, but couldn't even say the word and had to spell it out. You so wanted to be like the other guys your age who were interested in girls. Every time I read about a teen or a young adult who committed suicide because he or she couldn't accept being gay and was bullied about it, I felt afraid for you. Everyone has to work out and become comfortable with their sexual identity.

From all the research I've recently read, individuals on the autism spectrum are more vulnerable to having sexual development issues because of difficulties in acquiring social and sexual experience. I wish this subject had been better understood by the professionals who treated you over the years and had been discussed more in the ASD [autism spectrum disorder] literature. It seems to me that more understanding and conversation about sexual development for those on the autism spectrum would help others avoid some of the pain that you have had to experience in your life.

Nick: What have you learned are the best and worst things to say or do when I'm depressed?

Mom: The most important thing I've learned is not to try to talk to you about something until you are ready. That was true 20 years ago, and it is still true today. When I used to see that you were depressed, I wanted to deal with it immediately. I would get frustrated that you wouldn't talk about it right away, so I tried to force you to tell me what was wrong, which only made matters worse. Your dad is the same way in that he is not always ready to talk about what's bothering him. Sometimes it takes longer for him to process what's going on internally, so maybe that's just more of a male thing.

I believe the best thing to do when someone you care about is depressed is to really listen to them. My impulse was usually to try to fix the problem and make it go away. Quick. Put a bandage on it. Stop the pain. But that doesn't often work. Letting you know I really heard you was the most effective thing I could do, but I didn't always remember to do it.

Some important things to keep in mind about listening: don't be doing other things like cooking dinner, cleaning the house, or watching television at the same time you are listening to your children. Honor their feelings by being totally present. Then mirror what they have told you. Reflect it back to them so they know you heard them. Just the simple act of listening can be a soothing balm over a raw wound and a much better approach than trying to solve the problem.

The worst things to do were rushing you to talk before you were ready and not really listening but, instead, trying to solve the problem.

Dad: That's a very difficult question. There's not much I could ever say or do to make your depression go away. I've learned that the best things I can do are to patiently listen to your feelings, not offer quick solutions, and to tell you how much I value and love you. Of course, I can also support you by helping you get the professional help you need. The worst thing I can do is to say, "Don't feel depressed."

Nick: What have been the most useful strategies or approaches you have tried in helping me cope with depression during different stages of my life?

Mom: Some things have not changed over time. Like listening. No matter if you were 5, 15, or 25, it is still the best way to respond to you initially when you are depressed. Also waiting until you are ready to talk is still a good rule of thumb. I also think a positive approach was hearing us share personal stories, especially from Dad, about when he was growing up and had experiences similar to yours. I know it made you feel better when Dad talked about teachers not being able to decipher his handwriting either.

When you were younger, I was more proactive when you were depressed. I could make you do things you didn't want to do, like attend that social skills group, for which you will probably never forgive me. Now there is nothing I can make you do. As it should be, your happiness is your responsibility.

Dad: There have been a number of them, but only you can speak to their usefulness. Some examples would be:

- encouraging you to seek professional help

- reaffirming my love for you

- listening non-judgmentally to what you are willing to share about your depression

- spending time with you, doing activities that you enjoy.

Nick: How do you feel about antidepressants?

Mom: Like most parents, I was originally against any type of medication, but when your first depression went on and on, I was willing to give it a try. Now, I have no problem whatsoever with antidepressants. The most important question for parents to ask themselves is: "Will it help my child?", not "Will it reflect badly on me as a parent to have my child on medication?"

Dad: I believe antidepressants have their place as a legitimate modality in the treatment of depression. A competent doctor must determine and monitor the best course of action to take with respect to medications. It is equally important to be in therapy while taking medication to maximize its benefits.

Nick: How do you feel when you see I am depressed?

Mom: Helpless. I want to make it go away! But I have learned that the pain won't go away until you are ready to confront it, and there's not much I can say or do that will hasten that process along.

Dad: I feel great pain when you are in a depression. It is a feeling of total helplessness. I would do anything in my power to bring joy and happiness into your life.

Nick: What was the worst depression I've ever been in? What was it like for you?

Mom: For me, I think the worst episode of depression was when you went away to college because Dad and I weren't there to comfort or soothe you. You were only three hours away, and it was difficult for all of us. The thing that made it the worst was that for the first time, you talked about not wanting to live. Hearing that made me feel like I was falling out of a plane. It was terrifying, and to have you be three hours away made it even worse.

Dad: The worst depression was when you weren't able to complete your student teaching. Your sense of hopelessness was palpable. The fact that you have been able to scale that mountain and end up on the other side is remarkable and speaks to your inner strength.

Nick: Mom, as a former therapist yourself, what kind of therapist do you think is best for a child, adolescent, or young adult with Aspergers?

Mom: Here would be my three major criteria:

1. I think parents need to feel comfortable with their child's therapist. If something about the therapist creates discomfort of any kind, I would not send your child to that person. Often, therapists came highly recommended to us by other professionals or people we knew, but if something in our gut didn't feel right, we looked for someone else.

2. The child, adolescent, or young adult must feel comfortable working with that therapist. I don't think parents should ever force children to work with someone to whom their child can't comfortably talk.

3. Even if a therapist does not have a specialty in Asperger's or autism, he or she should at least be willing to get up to speed on the subject.

Nick: If a child is depressed, how long should parents wait before seeking professional help?

Mom: That's hard to say. It depends on the symptoms a child is demonstrating. Obviously, if a child is talking about not wanting to live, don't wait another minute. If a child is continually sad or angry, I would seek help, but it is often difficult to get your child to agree to see a therapist and you don't want to have to battle every week to get your child to go.

Dad: I would say there is no reason to hold off at all. My advice would be to act immediately and set up an appointment with a therapist, psychiatrist, or any combination thereof. Getting an early jump on things is better than getting too late a start.

Nick: What is your own personal way of dealing with depression?

Mom: I am very proactive when it comes to depression or anything else for that matter. I am a "Let's take care of business now before the situation gets any worse" kind of person. Most of the time, I believe that's a good thing but occasionally you just have to give a situation time and it will work itself out.

Dad: I do a number of things to feel as good as I can about my life and avoid feeling depressed. First, I believe that daily exercise is a great antidepressant. Every morning, I run outside for four miles and on some days I also work out at a gym. This daily ritual helps release any fear and anxiety I am feeling and is as beneficial as the physical benefits of exercise. Second, I try to eat a reasonably healthy diet. When my weight is at a good place and I'm eating nutritious foods, I feel better. Third, I have given a lot of thought to the way I view life. In Buddhist terms, I try to live in the moment. I plan for the future but don't worry about things over which I have no control. Some days I'm more successful than others in remembering that perspective.

Nick: You and Dad seem have to have different styles of coping with depression. Is that right?

Mom: That's for sure. Dad is more of a "wait and see" type of person. I think our approaches have been complementary where you are concerned. He might have the tendency to wait too long to address a problem and I might step in too soon. Between the two of us, we usually arrived at a happy medium.

Dad: I'm sure that's true. We are very different people with different coping mechanisms. Mom relies on introspection and talking to friends. I rely more on exercise. Even though I acknowledge that we have different ways of coping with depression, my way fits me but is certainly not the right way, the best way, or the only way. It simply works for me.

Nick: Can you talk about the experience I had with group therapy when I was in sixth and seventh grades?

Mom: Must I? Okay, I will… I admit this was the one and only time that Dad and I put a lot of pressure on you to meet with a particular therapist you didn't like and to be in a social skills group with other kids. We said if you went once and didn't like it, you didn't have to go back again. Well, you went once and hated it, but we reneged on our offer. To say you didn't want to attend these sessions is a cosmic understatement. For over a year, every week would be World War III before you went to those sessions. The therapist told us we shouldn't allow you to manipulate us into letting you off the hook so we held firm. But looking back on it, I'm not sure that was a good idea.

Dad: You hated group therapy. You felt that you were in a group of losers and you didn't belong in that category. You were only about 12 at the time and perhaps couldn't recognize that the group could be helpful to you. You wanted to hang out with the more popular kids and not be identified as an outsider. So being in that group threatened your identity. You didn't want to be one of them. I think you now have a more mature view on why being in that group was such an explosive issue for you.

Nick: Having met with a number of therapists over the years, what is the best way to shop for one?

Mom: Shopping is the operative word. Just because someone has been recommended to you doesn't necessarily mean you have to go with that person. And I don't think you have to spend a lot of money having sessions with different therapists in order to find one you and your child both like. I believe you can learn a lot about a therapist in a brief phone conversation in which you have a list of questions right in front of you and try to get a feel for that person. If the therapist will only answer these questions in person, move on to someone else.

Talking on the phone isn't always sufficient to make a decision. I remember one psychologist who sounded great on the phone, but in person he came across liked a used car salesman trying to sell us on what a great a therapist he was. But I think you can weed out the stinkers fairly easily in a short period of time. I remember calling one psychologist and was describing what had been recently going on, and he said, "Oh, I feel so sorry for you." He was history!

Dad: Get a good recommendation and then interview that person. After a few sessions, if a rapport hasn't been established, find someone else.

Nick: Looking back, is there anything you would have done differently in regards to my depression?

Mom: I'm sure there are many things, but I don't look back and feel guilty. I believe people can only do what they know at the time, and in that regard I did my best.

Dad: I wish we had known then what we know now—that you had Asperger's. It would have made us more conscious that your depression was based, in part, on your neurology rather than only on your psychology.

Afterword

Since I wrote this book in 2010, I have gone through the greatest depression of my life. I have written about this experience in my forthcoming book, *The Autism Spectrum, Sexuality and the Law*, co-authored with Drs. Tony Attwood and Isabelle Henault.

Appendix I

A List of
Recommended Books

Feeling Good by David Burns
An excellent introduction to cognitive–behavioral therapy techniques written specifically for the layperson.

Emotional Intelligence: Why it Can Matter More than IQ by Daniel Goleman
This book helps to explain the biological basis for emotions and how they can be consciously controlled.

The Complete Guide to Asperger's Syndrome by Tony Attwood
The "bible" of Asperger syndrome and a great resource to help someone with Asperger's gain self-understanding.

Asperger's from the Inside Out by Michael John Carley
The best guidebook for a newly diagnosed adult with Asperger syndrome, bar none.

Overcoming Depression by Paul Gilbert
A compassionate book on managing symptoms of depression, written by an expert clinician.

Transforming Depression by Doc Childre and Deborah Rozman
An important book to help understand the physiological connections between stress, depression, and the body. Terrific tips on managing depression using a holistic and unique approach called the HeartMath Solution.

Necessary Losses by Judith Viorst
This book changed my life. It helped me to understand and come to terms with mourning the losses of my past, which facilitated healing.

Undoing Depression by Richard O'Connor
This insightful book was written by a clinician who has suffered from depression.

Aspie Self-check List

After I received my diagnosis back in 2004, I made a list of the various AS traits I felt characterized who I was. How many traits do you share with me?

The characteristics listed below are simply Asperger's traits that I display. By no means do they represent a clinical basis for a diagnosis of Asperger's. To be sure of any diagnosis, contact a mental health practitioner.

General

☐ 1. I feel incompatible with the culture into which I was born. I feel culturally illiterate. That is, I do not know what movies are currently showing and do not really care. I do not like the current pop music of the day. My musical tastes are different from most people my age.

☐ 2. I often feel if I cannot be the best at what I attempt, I shouldn't attempt it at all.

☐ 3. Multitasking is almost impossible for me.

☐ 4. I crave positions of control and responsibility because I hate being told what to do, but I worry that I do not have the necessary abilities to handle such a job of authority.

☐ 5. Authenticity is vitally important to me.

THE AUTISM SPECTRUM AND DEPRESSION

☐ 6. The idea of a menial job in which I cannot express my creativity is unappealing to me.

☐ 7. If I'm going to do a job, I get the job done right, although it might take longer than expected.

☐ 8. I cannot start another project until I finish the one I am currently working on.

☐ 9. As a baby, as a young child, and even today, I was and am especially finicky about certain foods.

☐ 10. I am a perfectionist.

☐ 11. I find dates (calendars) to be fascinating. I like to know when things occurred.

☐ 12. I am fascinated with how things change over time.

☐ 13. I usually have a one-track mind.

☐ 14. I often lack common sense when it comes to everyday tasks that seem easy for others.

☐ 15. I have a problem understanding what is important and what is not.

☐ 16. I have difficulty generalizing information from one experience to another.

☐ 17. Even though I have high standards for people, I often tend to trust too easily.

☐ 18. When I am aware of the rules, I bend over backwards not to break them.

☐ 19. I am one of the most ethical people I know.

☐ 20. In the past, I was diagnosed with other existing co-morbidities.

□ 21. A member of my immediate family has been diagnosed with an autism spectrum disorder (or one of the other diagnoses listed above).

Emotions

□ 22. I am serious most of the time. People have often told me to lighten up.

□ 23. After a long day of expending energy, I need lots of down time.

□ 24. I have a temper that can come out at unexpected times.

□ 25. I need things to be a certain way, and I will literally go into a meltdown state if they are not the way I want them. Relatively small problems throughout the course of a day can send me into a meltdown state—a flat tire, flight delays at the airport, a restaurant being out of a certain food, and so on.

□ 26. I hate transitions throughout the course of a day.

□ 27. I dislike unpredictability. I like order and structure and often need it.

□ 28. I often feel there is a huge dichotomy within myself because although I consider myself creative, I am extremely rigid.

□ 29. If I do not show empathy, I feel it is not because I do not want to be empathetic, but it's genuinely because I missed an important piece of information.

□ 30. Nothing makes me angrier than injustice.

□ 31. Separating from my parents was or is a very difficult thing for me.

□ 32. My childhood went by too quickly. I do not feel ready to tackle the real world.

☐ 33. I do not like the idea of drinking alcohol or taking non-prescribed drugs because I want to be in control of my own behavior. I do not like the idea of being controlled by any substance.

☐ 34. I would hate to be hypnotized because the idea of someone controlling my behavior is unacceptable.

Academics

☐ 35. As a child, I found school activities such as handwriting, art, and physical education very laborious.

☐ 36. In school, I tended to tune out what I was not interested in.

☐ 37. I received some special education services as a child.

☐ 38. I attended a university. If I hadn't, I would have wanted to be able to.

☐ 39. I am more of a thinker than a feeler.

☐ 40. I tend to be a visual learner.

☐ 41. I tend to have trouble with visual–spatial processing.

☐ 42. I consider myself somewhat intelligent but lacking in social intelligence.

☐ 43. I pride myself on what I know, not on who I know.

☐ 44. I often feel like the comeback kid, in that I learn things a bit later than others, but once I do, I embrace it fully.

Language—Speech-processing

☐ 45. I find it difficult to pick up the general theme or plot of most movies I watch.

☐ 46. It takes me a few extra seconds to process what the other person has said before I can give a meaningful response. This is often frustrating for me because it seems like others can respond much more quickly than I can.

☐ 47. As a child, I had a speech delay but quickly caught up to age-appropriate levels.

☐ 48. I rarely lie, and if I do, it is extremely uncomfortable.

☐ 49. I do not understand the point of small talk.

☐ 50. I have a large vocabulary and tend to use big words during informal conversations. As a child, I sounded like a little professor because I was so articulate for my age

☐ 51. I have a sense of humor, but it is different from that of most people. I find puns and word-based humor funny.

☐ 52. I am often literal and do not understand social nuance.

☐ 53. I often talk to myself when I'm in a panic.

☐ 54. If I am presented with a complicated task, I need step-by-step instructions, otherwise I just can't perform the task.

☐ 55. I have trouble reading the body language of other people and judging intent.

Sensory

☐ 56. I have trouble when it comes to taking note of everything that is going on in my immediate environment. Normally I tend to focus on one or two things at a time.

☐ 57. My five senses are extremely sensitive.

☐ 58. If my senses are being bombarded with too much input, I will go into shutdown mode.

☐ 59. I have difficulty judging height, distance, and depth.

Social relationships

☐ 60. I often feel like I suffer from social fatigue syndrome.

☐ 61. Socializing is harder and takes more effort for me than academic tasks that interest me.

☐ 62. I often wish there were a textbook on the various pragmatics and the unwritten rules of social interaction because it does not come naturally for me. School was lacking for me in this area.

☐ 63. I identify more with a generation other than my own (i.e. people older or younger than myself).

☐ 64. I tend to be a loner.

☐ 65. Sometimes people tell me that I am in my own little world.

☐ 66. I am fairly immune to peer pressure.

☐ 67. I strongly dislike competition.

☐ 68. I love helping others.

☐ 69. I love teaching others what I know.

☐ 70. I am extremely loyal to my family.

☐ 71. I sometimes have trouble recognizing people.

☐ 72. To me, exchanging pleasantries with people I do not like feels fake and is extremely uncomfortable.

☐ 73. I find most people confusing.

☐ 74. I connect easier to animals than to humans.

☐ 75. People could take advantage of me because I am not assertive.

☐ 76. I often found it hard to deal with bullies because I did not have the social skills to befriend them or to defend myself.

☐ 77. I tend to either really like people or dislike them. With me, there is no in between.

☐ 78. People have to meet my integrity standards before I can decide whether I like them.

☐ 79. I dislike parties.

☐ 80. If someone is going to be my friend, he or she must meet my standards of honesty, integrity, and authenticity.

☐ 81. I do better at individual sports than team sports.

☐ 82. Sometimes I feel my social difficulties go unrecognized because I have learned to fake it, at least for a while.

☐ 83. Sometimes I have trouble knowing whether someone perceives me as a friend or just an acquaintance.

☐ 84. Sometimes I unconsciously tend to do things in public that are inappropriate, for example pick my nose, clean my ear canal, or put my coat on backwards.

☐ 85. Fashion is not that important to me.

☐ 86. I do not have great personal hygiene habits.

☐ 87. I am punctual.

☐ 88. I am uncomfortable dealing with those in authority.

Motor skills

☐ 89. I have fine motor difficulties. Using silverware, writing with a pencil, and doing things that involve the use of my hands is extremely challenging for me.

☐ 90. Gross motor skills present great difficulty for me. Throwing a ball and catching it, lifting weights, throwing a shot put, and other activities that involve larger muscle groups is extremely challenging for me.

☐ 91. I am relatively uncoordinated.

Interests

☐ 92. I have a large music and book collection.

☐ 93. I hate not being an expert in what I am interested in. I equate it with social incompetence.

☐ 94. I have several collections—coin collection, music collection, baseball card collection, collect statistics on a certain subject, and so on.

☐ 95. My expertise in areas of interest far outweighs my general knowledge about the world. I sometimes do not keep track of current world affairs because all of my time is spent learning more about my special interests.

☐ 96. I either share too much about what interests me, or I share too little.

☐ 97. I rarely read fiction books. I almost always read nonfiction.

References

Agassi, A. (2009) *Open: An Autobiography*. New York, NY: First Vintage Books.

Ansbacher, H. and Ansbacher, R. (1964) *The Individual Psychology of Alfred Adler: A Systematic Presentation in Selections from His Writings*. New York, NY: HarperCollins.

Armstrong, T. (2010) *Neurodiversity: Discovering the Extraordinary Gifts of Autism, ADHD, Dyslexia, and Other Brain Differences*. Philadelphia, PA: Da Capo Press.

Asperger's Association of New England (2013) "FAQs." Available at www.aane.org/about_asperger_syndrome/asperger_faqs.html, accessed on 10 October 2013.

Attwood, T. (2008) *The Complete Guide to Asperger's Syndrome*. London: Jessica Kingsley Publishers.

Berard, G. and Brockett, S. (2000) *Hearing Equals Behavior. The Daring New Program*. Schaumberg, IL: Ebooks2go.

Blackwell Publishing Ltd. (2006). 'Listening to music can reduce chronic pain and depression by up to a quarter.' *ScienceDaily* May 24. Available at www.sciencedaily.com/releases/2006/05/060524123803.htm, accessed on 11 October 2013.

Blaydes, J. (2003) *The Educator's Book of Quotes*. Los Angeles, CA: Corwin Press.

Bordowitz, H. (2006) *Billy Joel: The Life and Times of an Angry Young Man*. New York, NY: Billboard Books.

Brampton, S. (2008) *Shoot the Damn Dog: A Memoir of Depression*. New York, NY: W. W. Norton and Company, Inc.

Bruni, O., Ferri, R., Vittori, E., Novelli, L. *et al.* (2007) 'Sleep architecture and NREM alterations in children and adolescents with Asperger syndrome.' *Sleep 30*, 11, 1577–1585.

Burns, D. (1980) *Feeling Good: The New Mood Therapy*. New York, NY: William Morrow and Company.

Campbell, D. (1997) *The Mozart Effect: Tapping the Power of Music to Heal the Body, Strengthen the Mind, and Unlock the Creative Spirit*. New York, NY: HarperCollins.

Carley, M. J. (2008) *Asperger's from the Inside Out: A Supportive and Practical Guide for Anyone with Asperger's Syndrome*. New York, NY: Perigree.

Childre, D. and Rozman, D. (2007) *Transforming Depression: The HeartMath Solution to Feeling Overwhelmed, Sad, and Stressed.* Oakland, CA: New Harbinger Publications.

Cohen, D. (1995) *Out of the Blue: Depression and Human Nature.* New York, NY: W. W. Norton and Company, Inc.

Cousens, G. (2000) *Depression-Free for Life: A Physician's All-Natural 5-Step Plan.* New York, NY: HarperCollins.

Delong, R. G. and Dwyer, J. T. (1988) "Correlation of family history with specific autistic subtypes: Asperger syndrome and bipolar affective disease." *Journal of Autism and Development Disorders 18*, 593–600.

Dubin, N. (2007) *Asperger Syndrome and Bullying: Strategy and Solutions.* London: Jessica Kingsley Publishers.

Dubin, N. (2009) *Asperger Syndrome and Anxiety: A Guide to Successful Stress Management.* London: Jessica Kingsley Publishers.

Ellis, A. and Harper, R. (1975) *A Guide to Rational Living.* Chatsworth, CA: Wilshire Books.

Erikson, E. (1959) *Identity and the Life Cycle.* New York, NY: W. W. Norton and Company, Inc.

Farb, N. A., Anderson, A. K., Mayberg, H., Bean, J. *et al.* (2010) "Minding one's emotions: Mindfulness training alters the neural expression of sadness." *Emotion 10*, 1, 25–33.

Frankl, V. (1959) *Man's Search for Meaning.* Boston, MA: Beacon Press.

Gaylin, W. (1983) *Psychodynamic Understanding of Depression: The Meaning of Despair.* Northvale, NJ: J. Aronson.

Germain, A. and Kupfer, D. J. (2008) "Circadian rhythm disturbances in depression." *Human Psychopharmacology* (October) *23*, 7, 571–85.

Ghaziuddin, M. (2005) *Mental Health Aspects of Autism and Asperger Syndrome.* London: Jessica Kingsley Publishers.

Ghaziuddin, M. and Greden, J. (1998) 'Depression in children with autism/pervasive developmental disorders: a case-control family history study.' *Journal of Autism and Developmental Disorders 28*, 111–115.

Gillberg, C. (2002) *A Guide to Asperger Syndrome.* Cambridge: Cambridge University Press.

Goleman, D. (1999) *Emotional Intelligence: Why it Can Matter More than IQ.* New York, NY: Bantham Hardcover.

Grof, S. and Grof, C. (1992) *The Stormy Search for the Self: A Guide to Personal Growth through Transformational Crisis.* New York, NY: Tarcher/Penguin.

Horney, K. (1950) *Neurosis and Human Growth: The Struggle Toward Self-Realization.* New York, NY: W. W. Norton.

Howlin, P. (2005) "Outcomes in autism spectrum disorders." In F. R. Volkmar, R. Paul, A. Klin, and D.J. Cohen (eds) *Handbook of Autism and Pervasive Developmental Disorders.* Hoboken, NJ: Wiley.

Kambara, M. and Sakamoto, S. (1998) 'A longitudinal study of the relationship between attributional style, life events, and depression in Japanese undergraduates.' *Journal of Social Psychology 138*, 2, 229–240.

Katie, B. (2003) *Loving What Is: Four Questions That Can Change Your Life.* New York, NY: Three Rivers Press.

Kramer, P. (2005) *Against Depression.* New York, NY: Penguin.

Kurtz, E. and Ketcham, K. (1993) *The Spirituality of Imperfection: Storytelling and the Journey to Wholeness.* New York, NY: Bantam Books.

Lerner, M. J. (1980) *The Belief in a Just World: A Fundamental Delusion.* New York, NY: Plenum Press.

Levitin, D. (2007) *This Is Your Brain on Music: The Science of a Human Obsession.* New York, NY: Penguin.

Lipton, B. and Bhaerman, S. (2009) *Spontaneous Evolution: Our Positive Future and a Way to Get There From Here.* Carlsbad, CA: Hay House.

Lowen, A. (1972) *Depression and the Body.* New York: Arcane.

Lynn, G. (2007) *The Asperger Plus Child: How to Identify and Help Children with Asperger Syndrome and Seven Common Co-Existing Conditions.* Shawnee Mission, KS: Autism-Asperger Publishing Company.

Mays, J. B. (1999) *In the Jaws of the Black Dogs: A Memoir of Depression.* New York, NY: HarperCollins.

Mental Health Today (no date) "DSM IV: Major Depressive Episode." Available at www.mental-health-today.com/dep/dsm.htm, accessed on 10 October 2013.

Mondimore, F. (2006) *Depression, The Mood Disease* (3rd edn.). Baltimore, MD: The Johns Hopkins University Press.

Moore, T. (2004) *Dark Nights of the Soul: A Guide to Finding Your Way Through Life's Ordeals.* New York, NY: Penguin.

Morris, S. and Kanfer, F. (1983) "Altruism and depression." *Personality Sociology Psychology Bulletin 9*, 567–577.

Murphy, D. G., Daly, E., Schmitz, N., Toal, F. *et al.* (2006) "Cortical serotonin 5-HT2A receptor binding and social communication in adults with Asperger's syndrome: an in vivo SPECT study." *The American Journal of Psychiatry* (May) *163*, 5, 934–936.

O'Connor, R. (2010) *Undoing Depression: What Therapy Can't Teach You and Medication Can't Give You.* New York, NY: The Berkley Publishing Group.

Ozment, J. and Lester, D. (1998) "Suicidality and helplessness." *Psychological Reports* (October) *83*, 2, 718.

Papolos, D and Papolos, J. (1997) *Overcoming Depression* (3rd edn). New York, NY: HarperCollins.

Parker-Pope, T. (2008) "Using music to lift depresssion's veil." Available at http://well.blogs.nytimes.com/2008/01/24/using-music-to-lift-depressions-veil, accessed on 10 October 2013.

Phillips, A. (2008) "Asperger's therapy hits Second Life." *ABC News* 10 Jan. Available at http://abcnews.go.com/Technology/OnCall/story?id=4133184&page=1, accessed on 11 October 2013.

Sacks, O. (2008) *Musicophilia: Tales of Music and the Brain* (revised and expanded edn.). New York, NY: Random House.

Schwartz, J. (2003) *The Mind and the Brain: Neuroplasticity and the Power of Mental Force.* New York, NY: Harper Perennial.

Shore, S. (2006) *Understanding Autism for Dummies.* Indianapolis, IN: Wiley Publishing.

Shore, S. (2013) "True inclusion through music." *Autism Asperger's Digest* (May–June), 36–39.

Siegal, A. (1996) *Heinz Kohut and the Psychology of the Self.* London: Routledge.

Solomon, A. (2001) *The Noonday Demon: An Atlas of Depression.* New York, NY: Scribner.

Stoddart, K. (2005) *Children, Youth and Adults with Asperger Syndrome: Integrating Multiple Perspectives.* London: Jessica Kingsley Publishers.

Styron, W. (1990) *Darkness Visible: A Memoir of Madness.* New York, NY: Random House.

Van Zomeren, M. and Lodewijkx, H. F. M. (2009) "'Could it be me?' Threat-related state orientation increases position identification with innocent victims." *European Journal of Social Psychology 39*, 223–236.

Vickerstaff, S., Heriot, S., Wong, M., Lopes, A. and Dossetor, D. (2006) "Intellectual ability, self-perceived social competence and depressive symptomatology in children with high-functioning autistic spectrum disorders." *Australian Journal of Psychology: Combined Abstracts of 2006 Australian Psychology Conferences, 58* (s2006), 202.

Viorst, J. (2003) *Necessary Losses: The Loves, Illusions, Dependencies, and Impossible Expectations that All of Us Have to Give Up in Order to Grow.* New York, NY: Fireside.

Whitfield, C. (1987) *Healing the Child Within: Discovery and Recovery for Adult Children of Dysfunctional Families.* Deerfield Beach, FL: Health Communications.

Whitfield, C. (2003) *The Truth about Depression: Choices for Healing.* Deerfield Beach, FL: Health Communications.

Williams, D. (1999) *Nobody Nowhere: The Extraordinary Autobiography of an Autistic.* London: Jessica Kingsley Publishers.

Williams, D. (2002) *Exposure Anxiety: The Invisible Cage: An Exploration of Self-Protection Responses in the Autism Spectrum and Beyond.* London: Jessica Kingsley Publishers.

Wrongplanet.net (2008) "How many times per week do you think about death and dying?" Available at www.wrongplanet.net/postt55551.html, accessed on 11 October 2013.

Yapko, M. (1997) *Breaking the Patterns of Depression.* New York, NY: Doubleday.

Young, J., Klosko, J. and Weishaar, M. (2003) *Schema Therapy: A Practitioner's Guide.* New York, NY: Guilford Press.

Index

adolescence 44–7
Agassi, Andre 140
Alder, Alfred 141
altruism 34–5
American Psychological Association 72, 89
"Angel Animals and Autistics: A Love Affair" (Dubin) 162–5
anger 147–54
Ansbacher, H. 141
Ansbacher, R. 141
"Art of Self-Disclosure, The" (Dubin) 177–80
Asperger syndrome
    and adolescence 44–7
    altruism of 34–5
    and anger 147–9, 152–3
    and bipolar depression 77–9
    and "dark night of the soul" 124–32
    diagnosis of 32
    empathy in 29–30, 31–3
    employment 175–7
    and "The Greatness of Asperger's" article 181–6
    group belonging 36–7
    and inner critic 59–62
    language delay 40
    link to depression 17–18
    as minority group 29–30, 31–3
    over-identification 31–3
    and perfectionism 139, 140, 142
    and psychosocial development 39–48
    school experiences 37–8, 41–4
    serotonin levels 70
    sexuality 45–6
    and sleep 70–1, 171
    and social networking sites 166–9
    and suicide 133

Asperger Syndrome and Anxiety (Dubin) 16, 63, 66, 83, 88, 96, 104, 182, 187
Asperger Syndrome and Bullying (Dubin) 187
Asperger's Association of New England 34
Asperger's and Self-Esteem: Insight and Hope Through Famous Roles Models (Ledgin) 183
Attwood, Tony 23, 40, 140, 148, 181
atypical depression 73–4

Beck, Aaron 96
Beethoven, Ludwig van 118–19
Bentley May, John 55
Berard, Guy 158
bipolar depression 74–9
Blaydes, J. 130
Bordowitz, H. 118
Brampton, Sally 54
Brockett, S. 158
Bruni, O. 71
Buddha 25–7, 34
Burns, David 88, 96–103
Bush, George W. 98–9
Byron, Lord 28, 75

Campbell, Don 158
Camus, Albert 28
Character Strengths and Virtues (Seligman and Peterson) 184–5
childhood trauma 71
Chopin, Frederic 75
cognitive–behavioral therapy (CBT) 83, 88
    and Albert Ellis 88–90
    books on 88
    and cognitive distortions 95–103
    description of 81–5
    and *Dr. Phil* show 95–6

cognitive–behavioral therapy (CBT) *cont.*
rational emotive behavioral therapy
89–90
and self-schemas 103–11
cognitive distortions 62–3, 95–103
Cohen, D. 28
Complete Guide to Asperger Syndrome, The
(Attwood) 23, 140, 148
Couric, Katie 131
Cousens, G. 69, 70
Csikszentmihalyi, Mihaly 182–3
cyclothymia 76–7

"dark night of the soul" 113–17, 119–21
and Asperger syndrome 124–32
in films 122–3
historical figures with 117–19
Darkness Visible (Styron) 57
dating 174–5
DeLong, R.G. 78
depression
and altruism 34–5
and anger 150–2, 153–4
atypical 73–4
bipolar 74–9
and childhood trauma 71
description of 49
dysthymic 72–3
feelings of 54–7
genetic role in 71
group belonging 36
inner critic during 57–63
learned helplessness in 63–8
and life transitions 50–3
link to Asperger syndrome 17–18
management of 155–86
manic 74–9
neurons and neurotransmitters in 68–70
ontological rejection 74
and perfectionism 139–45
Siddhartha's experience of 25–7, 34
and sleep 57–8, 70–1, 171–3
therapists for 169–70
triggers for 50–3
types of 71–7
and vitamins 70
see also management of depression
depressive realism 28–9
Diagnosing Jefferson (Ledgin) 183
*Diagnostic and Statistical Manual of Mental
Disorders* (DSM-IV) 32, 72, 181
"Discovery of 'Aspie' Criteria, The" (Attwood
and Gray) 181

Dr. Phil show 95–6
dopamine 69
Dubin, Nick 165
with Asperger syndrome 127, 128,
129–30, 194
and CBT 83, 88
at college 192–3
"dark night of the soul" experience
113–17, 119–21, 127, 128
early experience of depression 18–20,
188–201
feelings of depression 55–7
inner critic 57–62, 85–6
interview with parents 187–201
language delay 40
learned helplessness 66, 67–8
management of depression 155–6,
159–60, 161–6, 176, 177–80,
194–201
motor skills 41
on music 161–2
perfectionism of 139, 140–1, 142–4
on pets 162–5
at school 37–8, 42, 45, 189–92
on self-disclosure 177–80
self-schemas 105–7, 108–11
sexuality 194–5
on social networking 168–9
spiritual crisis 116–17
suicidal thoughts 78–9
Dwyer, J.T. 78
Dyer, Wayne 33
dysthymic depression 72–3

Edison, Thomas 77
Ellis, Albert 88–90, 96, 106
empathy 29–30, 31–3
employment 175–7
Erickson, Erik 39, 42
Erikson, Milton 82
exercise 173
exposure anxiety 58

Farb, N.A. 157
Feeling Good (Burns) 88, 96–103
feelings of depression 54–7
Fitzgerald, Michael 183
Flow: The Psychology of Optimal Experience
(Csikszentmihalyi) 182–3
Frankl, Victor 21, 117
Freud, Sigmund 62

Gaylin, W. 60
genetics 71
Genius Genes: How Asperger Talents Changed the World (Fitzgerald) 183
Germain, A. 70
Ghaziuddin, M. 49
Gillberg, C. 133
global statements 64–5
Gould, Glenn 77
gratitude 174
Gray, Carol 181
"Greatness of Asperger's, The" 181–6
Greden, J. 49
Grof, Christina 121
Grof, Stanislav 121
group belonging 36–7
Guide to Rational Living, A (Ellis and Harper) 96

Harper, R. 96
Healing the Child Within (Whitfield) 71
Hearing Equals Behavior (Berard and Brockett) 158
Holotropic Breathwork™ 121
Horney, Karen 97
Howlin, P. 133

In the Jaws of the Black Dogs: A Memoir of Depression (Bentley May) 55
inner critic 57–63, 85–6
It's a Wonderful Life 134–5

Joel, Billy 118
Jordon, Michael 131
Jung, Carl 128, 130

Kambara, M. 64
Kanfer, F. 34
Katie, Byron 90–5, 106
Keller, Helen 21
Kennedy, John F. 106
Ketcham, K. 140
Klosko, Jaanet 88
Kohut, Heinz 61
Kramer, Peter 28
Kupfer, D.J. 70
Kurtz, E. 140

language delay 40
learned helplessness 63–8
Ledgin, Norm 183
Lerner, M.J. 31
Lester, D. 64

Levitin, D. 158
life transitions 50–3
Lodewijkx, H.F.M. 31
Lowen, Alexander 54
lying 152
Lynn, G. 77, 78

management of depression 194–201
    dating 174–5
    employment 175–7
    exercise 173
    gratitude 174
    medication 155–7, 196–7
    mindfulness 157
    music 158–62
    pets 162–6
    self-consciousness 180
    self-disclosure 177–80
    sleep 70–1, 171–3
    social networking 166–9
    therapists 169–70, 198, 199–201
manic depression 74–9
Man's Search for Meaning (Frankl) 21
McCullough, Kathy 38
medication 155–7, 196–7
Mill, John Stuart 158–9
Mondimore, F. 53
Moore, T. 128
Morris, S. 34
Mozart Effect, The (Campbell) 18
Murphy, D.G. 70
music 158–62
"Music and Moods" (Dubin) 161–2

neurons 68–70
neurotransmitters 68–70
Nobody Nowhere: The Extraordinary Autobiography of an Autistic (Williams) 58
Noonday Demon, The (Solomon) 54
norepinephrine 69

Obama, Barack 29, 99
O'Connor, R. 94
ontological rejection 74
Open: An Autobiography (Agassi) 140
over-identification 31–3
Ozment, J. 64

Papolos, D. 63
Papolos, J. 63
Parker-Pope, T. 158
perfectionism 139–45, 149

personal identifications 31–3
pessimism 28–9
Peterson, Christopher 184–5
pets 162–6
Phillips, A. 167
positional identifications 31–3
psychosocial development, theory of 39–48

Rado, Sandor 60
rational emotive behavioral therapy (REBT)
    89–90, 106
Rogers, Carl 130

Sacks, O. 159
St. John of the Cross 117
Sakamoto, S. 64
Sampras, Pete 130–1
Schema Therapy (Young, Klosko, and
    Weishaar) 88
school 37–8, 41–4, 45
Schwartz, J. 96
self-consciousness 180
self-disclosure 177–80
self-schemas 103–11
Seligman, Martin 184–5
serotonin 69–70
sexuality 45–6
Shoot the Damn Dog (Brampton) 54
Shore, Stephen 159
Siddhartha 25–7, 34
Siegal, A. 61
sleep
    and Asperger syndrome 70–1, 171
    and management of depression 70–1,
        171–3
    as symptom of depression 57–8
"Social Cyberspace" (Dubin) 168–9
social networking sites 166–9
Solomon, Andrew 54
Spirituality of Imperfection, The: Storytelling
    and the Search for Meaning (Kutrz and
    Ketcham) 140
Stoddart, K. 50–1, 124
Styron, William 57, 159
suicide 78–9, 133
    and Asperger syndrome 133
    and It's a Wonderful Life 134–5
    risk of 136
    steps to take 137–8
Sullivan, Annie 21
Suzuki, Shunryu 140
synaptic transmissions 68

Taylor, James 138
Tchiakovsky, Pyotr 75–6
therapists 169–70, 198, 199–201
Tolstoy, Leo 28
triggers for depression 50–3
Truman Show, The 122–3
Truth about Depression, The (Whitfield) 71

Van Zomeren, M. 31
Vickerstaff, S. 49
Vitamin D 70

Wallace, Mike 57
Weishaar, Marjorie 88
Whitfield, Charles 71
Williams, Donna 58
Wizard of Oz, The 122
"Work, The" process 90–5, 106

Yapko, M. 82
Young, Jeffery 88

The Autism Spectrum, Sexuality and the Law
What every parent and professional needs to know
Tony Attwood, Isabelle Hénault and Nick Dubin

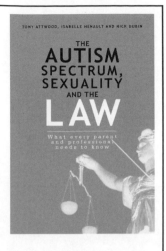

Based on Nick Dubin's own experience, and drawing on the extensive knowledge of Dr. Tony Attwood and Dr. Isabelle Hénault, this important book addresses the issues surrounding the autism spectrum (ASD), sexuality and the law

The complex world of sex and appropriate sexual behaviour can be extremely challenging for people with ASD and, without guidance, many find themselves in vulnerable situations. This book examines how the ASD profile typically affects sexuality and how sexual development differs between the general population and those with ASD. It explains the legalities of sexual behaviour, how laws differ from country to country, and the possibility for adjustment of existing laws as they are applied to the ASD population. With advice on how to help people with autism spectrum disorder gain a better understanding of sexuality and a comprehensive list of resources, the book highlights the need for a more informed societal approach to the psychosexual development of people with ASD.

A groundbreaking and honest account, this book will be an invaluable addition to the shelves of parents of children with ASD, mental health and legal professionals, teachers, carers and other professionals working with individuals on the spectrum.